Production Management and Control

Production Management and Control

Edited by
Vas Prabhu
Principal Lecturer in Production and Operations Management
Newcastle-upon-Tyne Polytechnic

and

Malcolm Baker
International Management Consultant and Director of Training
Institute of Production Control

McGRAW-HILL Book Company (UK) Limited

London · New York · St Louis · San Francisco · Auckland · Bogotá
Guatemala · Hamburg · Johannesburg · Lisbon · Madrid · Mexico
Montreal · New Delhi · Panama · Paris · San Juan · São Paulo
Singapore · Sydney · Tokyo · Toronto

Published by
McGRAW-HILL Book Company (UK) Limited
MAIDENHEAD · BERKSHIRE · ENGLAND

On behalf of the
Institute of Production Control
STRATFORD-UPON-AVON · WARWICKSHIRE · ENGLAND

British Library Cataloguing in Publication Data

Production management and control.
  1. Production management—Great Britain
  I. Prabhu, Vas II. Baker, Malcolm
  658.5′00941 TS155
  ISBN 0-07-084933-1

Library of Congress Cataloging-in-Publication Data

Prabhu, Vas
  Production management and control.
  1. Production management. 2. Production control.
  I. Baker, Malcolm. II. Title.
  TS155.P68 1986   658.5   85-10275
  ISBN 0-07-084933-1

12345 CUP89876

Typeset by Santype International Ltd, Salisbury, Wilts, and printed and bound in Great Britain at the University Press, Cambridge.

Contents

Preface

During the past decade we have all experienced ever increasing changes in the world. It is not just the political, social and economic changes which have a dramatic effect on society, but the rapid technological changes which are also taking place, linked with the ability to communicate quickly, travel to, and trade with different parts of the globe. The productive and effective use of our resources—manpower, materials, machinery and money—is becoming an essential ingredient for success. This book provides an insight into the ways in which these goals can be achieved through better planning and control. It is aimed at the practitioners in manufacturing industry who wish to enhance their understanding of this complex area of management by increasing their awareness of the concepts and principles involved in managing the manufacturing function. The book is also aimed at those embarking on a career in the production control and management field who would like to gain a basic understanding of the subject area early on in their work experience. The material presented in the book is relevant and appropriate to any type of manufacturing company whether it is producing furniture, textiles, petrochemicals, ceramics, pharmaceuticals, electronics, foods, etc., as well as being relevant to both the small and the large company. The book will also prove invaluable to academic tutors and training managers who are involved in the production management and control field.

The contents of this book are essentially drawn from course material that the Institute of Production Control has developed and used successfully on a whole range of short management courses that it runs for senior and middle management from manufacturing and service industries. The Institute felt that this material, though originally developed for use on its own seminars and short courses, would be of considerable interest and of potential use to the vast majority of production managers and their peers, who typically cannot or sometimes do not have the time to attend external daytime courses. In its attempt to reach as many industrial managers as possible, the Institute has therefore made its material available through this publication.

The subject matter has been grouped under five major headings (chapters). Chapter 1 provides an overview to the management aspects of production including a description of the complexity of this task. The relevance of certain industrial engineering tools in achieving this task is also explained. The next three chapters (2, 3 and 4) deal with the principal problem areas of production management and the ways in which they ought to be tackled for achieving high resource productivity and customer satisfaction. Chapter 2 looks at forecasting and production planning and aggregate and capacity planning in relation to planning manufacturing resources. Chapter 3 deals with the second important area, that of production control. Several key issues such as the function of production control, its organization for effective control, its systems and documentation are developed and explained. In Chapter 4 the focus of attention is on materials control. Besides introducing the concepts of modern materials management, this chapter develops the managerial aspects of inventory control and materials requirements planning. Finally, Chapter 5 is devoted to the important role of computers in production management. The appropriate choice of the computer, the impact of high technology and the kind of computerized systems used in manufacturing and physical distribution management are the topics developed in this chapter.

The book can be used by the potential reader in a number of ways. It could be read straight through from beginning to end, especially by the novice, in order to gain an overview on the major aspects of this function or it could be read on a selective basis by the more experienced practitioner, who may wish to increase his knowledge and understanding in specific areas of the manufacturing and service management task by referring only to those sections that he wishes.

Open learning is a highly cost-effective way of learning, allowing people to learn at a time, place and pace to suit their individual needs. This book will prove a valuable information resource in its own right to both companies and individuals involved with open learning projects. However, one point that every reader should bear in mind when reading this book, is the need to discuss the topics within it with colleagues at work or other interested persons, as often the learning process will be enhanced by trying to apply or even relate the theoretical concepts and principles to one's own working environment and experience. In this respect, if required, the Institute of Production Control would be willing to provide additional support

on an individual basis or through participation in its own training programmes. What this book has to offer to manufacturing industry applies
also to the processing industry.

K. Roberts
General Secretary

Discrimination between the sexes

In a book on this subject it has not been possible to eliminate the use of
gender and still retain a fluent text. A deliberate distinction between the
sexes is not implied.

Production management:
An overview

Production management is such a vast subject area covering so many diverse but interrelated functional areas that it is extremely difficult to describe the whole without having to divide it into discrete parts. This is in fact the basis on which the remaining chapters of this book have been structured. In this chapter, an attempt is made to present a broad overview of the managerial functions of production, highlighting the importance of several skills—technical, economic and behavioural—that a competent production manager would be expected to possess. Also the responsibilities of a typical production manager are presented to highlight the range of functions that he is normally expected to control and the sheer complexity of the nature of his work which is usually making optimum trade-offs between two or more conflicting objectives. The overall tasks of the production manager being such a complex one, the need for using appropriate managerial tools for achieving high productivity becomes of paramount importance. Several such tools are normally available to the production manager, but in this chapter the crucial role played by 'industrial engineering' techniques is described. Being such well-established techniques, it is absolutely essential that every production manager is not only aware of these techniques but also can apply them to raise or maintain his resource productivity levels.

1.1 Modern production management

The purpose of production management is that of organizing efficient manufacture of goods, whether these are products, parts, materials or other commodities. To achieve this, the basic resources of manufacture, the four

1

Ms—materials, machinery, manpower and money—have to be used effectively for the creation of wealth in society.

To be more specific, the overall goals or objectives should be the following:

1. To meet realistic *production plans.*
2. To achieve excellent *quality standards.*
3. Maximum *productivity.*
4. Good *human relationships.*

Each of these items will now be covered in more detail.

PRODUCTION PLANS

This means not only meeting delivery promises, but making realistic delivery promises as well. Very frequently companies will commit themselves to provide services which they have no chance of meeting, with the result that customers are let down and become disappointed at the least, or extremely irritated with the likelihood of going elsewhere for their needs. Today we are living in a very competitive world-wide market situation for many of our goods, and have to be as good as the best international company to compete effectively.

To achieve this efficient service from manufacturing, it demands that production control (PC) must be done effectively within the company. The following components are those of the PC function:

1. Demand forecasting.
2. Capacity or aggregate planning.
3. Detailed production planning.
4. Work scheduling.
5. Materials requirement planning.
6. Materials flow in processes.

Each of these components will be described in more detail later.

QUALITY STANDARDS

All too often in manufacturing, the least that will do is sufficient or 'what we can get away with'. Quality is something that has to be designed into a product or service from its conception to make sure that the potential customer has something that:

1. Will satisfy the function for which it was designed.
2. Looks attractive—a major selling consideration in most products.

3. Is easy to apply or use.
4. Is reliable.
5. Does not deteriorate quickly through poor finishing, poorly made materials, etc.

All these are aspects of quality.

Quality should be started at the design stage and should include the detailed specification of the goods to be manufactured, so that well-documented and realistic standards are set for materials, operations, the inspections that are necessary, and so on. The emphasis must be on 'zero defects', getting it 'right first time', and so on as with the following:

1. *Materials* Specify the materials needed in terms of national standards, codes, ingredients, tolerances, tests, etc. Quantify the amount of material for the particular product or part in terms of quantity per metre/kilo. Stipulate the sequence and flow for economical use of the materials, including utilization, coverage, identification, and testing stages.

2. *Operations* The detailed method for achieving the desired specification, dimensions, tolerances, finish required, specific technical or quality tests needed including operation lists, method specifications, inspections or test procedures, process quality, training procedures, etc.

Specific techniques and methodologies for improving quality must also be organized. These could include the following: Standard room procedures, 'quality circles', quality control organization and manning, incoming inspection routine, sampling and statistical quality control procedures and a quality improvement system (QIS) for operator training, setting standards and inspection/testing routines.

PRODUCTIVITY

Productivity is the ratio of input to output of whatever resources one is using; for instance these could be:

$$\text{Labour} = \frac{\text{output}}{\text{input}} = \frac{\text{(measured in standard hours)}}{\text{(measured in attendance hours)}}$$

$$\text{Machinery} = \frac{\text{output}}{\text{input}} = \frac{\text{(measured in machine running time)}}{\text{(machine available hours)}}$$

$$\text{Materials} = \frac{\text{output}}{\text{input}} = \frac{\text{(effective material usage)}}{\text{(starting quantity)}}$$

$$\text{Money} = \frac{\text{output}}{\text{input}} = \frac{\text{(cash flow over a given period)}}{\text{(investment)}}$$

3

The discipline whereby the productivity of a business is looked at as a specialized activity is *industrial engineering*, which is the subject of Sec. 1.4.

Included in productivity must be the productivity of finance where money is the medium of exchange. The discipline in this activity is that of management accounting, which comprises, among other things, the following:

1. *Standard costing*   Including marginal costing and direct costing.
2. *Budgetary control and cost control*   Including labour cost control and variance reporting.
3. *Profit planning*   Contribution statements, product-market revenues, operating statements, cash planning and controls.
4. *Financial modelling*   Market modelling, production models, profit and loss modelling, investment and cash flow forecast and 'what if' alterations.

HUMAN RELATIONSHIPS

With the wide-ranging activities of the behavioural sciences in recent years, there is a considerable body of knowledge of what ought to constitute the building blocks for improving human relationships, industrial relations and human development.

In fact, this is probably one of the most important areas of management activity; but it is also one of the most difficult areas to manage expertly.

Perhaps the main areas for consideration are the following:

1. People work better when they have specific goals for achievement in their work, often known as 'action plans'.
2. Building 'team working' groups is essential in a company.
3. The development of people in terms of skills, and in terms of character and rational/emotional development linked to inter-personal relationships is essential.
4. People matter as ends in themselves and not as means to an end.
5. The development of personal responsibility, self-enrichment and self-worth is important.

SUMMARY

The modern production manager requires many skills to perform his job satisfactorily; these are:

1. *Technical skills*   Engineering- or science-based knowledge; management techniques and systems.

4

2. *Economic skills* Evaluation/investment appraisal; cost control; budgeting

3. *Managerial skills* Behavioural/human relations; leadership; personnel development.

The appropriate skills and knowledge in each of these areas is necessary in production managers, who usually have responsibility for the greater number of people, the highest value of assets, and a wider range of activities than any other manager.

1.2 What is management?

We often have a better appreciation of what we are talking about if we can define our terms. Definitions need to be precise, but unfortunately this does not mean that everyone will have the same understanding, so therefore they at best give an approximation of the original thought.

A definition of management is that 'it is a creative activity which develops an organization and its people to achieve specific goals'. This needs explanation. What is meant by creative ability? How do we develop organizations and people? What is meant by specific goals? But it is sufficient to provide an initial understanding of the concept of management.

Creative here implies innovative design, bringing forth new thoughts, acquiring relevant knowledge.

An organization may have any of the following goals as overall objectives, but in every case they can be broken into many sub-objectives:

1. The provision of products or services to the community.

2. The economic and social wellbeing of a nation.

3. The search for and dissemination of knowledge.

4. The health care of people.

5. The worship of God.

Each of the organizations above is very different from one another. They may include manufacturing concerns, a nation, university, hospital complex and a church. Management and organization are necessary in each case. The more that goals and objectives are specific, the better.

Management styles within an organization will differ according to the personality and temperament of each individual manager and be influenced greatly by culture and beliefs and what motivates a person.

5

Management is often thought about in historical terms: scientific management as being an older concept, followed by behavioural management, and this followed by concepts of systems management, and so on. Perhaps the historical perceptions of management have come about in this way, but it is our belief that each of these different aspects of approach to management is relative and needs to be integrated.

Without scientific principles, management degenerates to acting on beliefs and feelings (which may be relevant), but in today's high technology society, this will just not do. Beliefs can be very different between individuals, and feelings are apt to change from day to day.

SCIENTIFIC MANAGEMENT

This implies analysis, measurement and methodology, and is essential in modern organizations in gaining insight and knowledge of a situation. It may not be total knowledge or complete insight, but without this kind of information, decisions tend to be made with inadequate data, and often the worst kind of decision is made. Some managers have often been accused of intransigence—'My mind is made up, don't confuse me with facts.'

We all have different perceptions of facts. For instance, physiologists will tell us that sight can be conceived as sensory perception through the eyes, through the cones and rods to signals received in the brain which are then interpreted by association. On the other hand, we are told by physiologists that we have to have some mental image to start with, and therefore two-way interaction between brain and eye messages is needed. Or further, we can see only what we expect to see, that is, the eyes are interpreters of what we already sense. Knowledge has many facets, according to where we start and how we look at events and things. Scientific knowledge is an important facet of knowledge which provides better insight.

Measured knowledge is not creative until that knowledge is 'synthesized', built into a coherent role. This is one aspect of what management is about.

Scientific knowledge is limited to that which is measurable or quantifiable. It is only part of total knowledge and is quite limited, but it is essential. Science and the use of science (called technology) has given us many advantages during this century—and some disadvantages. For instance, science and knowledge can be used for good or evil. Therefore discernment and judgement based on belief are necessary.

Science is based on belief—that we are living in an ordered and rational universe, and that there are natural laws to be discovered. It is further believed that companies would operate more effectively if they were more specific and scientific in their approach and outlook on business life.

6

BEHAVIOURAL MANAGEMENT

This is based on the fact that any organizational activity is a human enterprise, and that work is directed to human goals—certainly both manufacturing and service organizations serve human needs:

1. The customer benefits from the products or community service offered by an organization. Without human beings there would be no need for the organization to exist!

2. Organizations are providers of employment. Most of us have to work in order to live; some less fortunate have difficulty in obtaining work, occasionally because they have not wanted to adapt to new environments and skills, and more often because of trade recession, when whole classes of work have been made redundant.

Work has two advantages:

1. It provides a means of satisfaction for people who take pride in what they achieve. The craftsman working with his hands has many advantages over others in this respect, as has the person who serves others, such as in health care. Other people's work is intrinsically interesting— this is perhaps the area of the professional who is engrossed in his work where study, observation and practice are all involved with a desire to improve.

2. It provides the means of living. Work enables us to pay for our daily bread. Too many people today have over-emphasized this aspect of work, where the material rewards far outweigh the input. There is nothing wrong in having possessions, provided that they do not possess us.

The knowledge and conclusions of behavioural management are based on the findings of psychologists, physiologists and sociologists, which in turn are based on theories, empirical research and interpretations. These findings are useful in that the pattern of behaviour for social groupings can be known and used 'creatively' for furthering the goals of the enterprise.

They do not, however, show how individuals or groups will always behave in the future. Each individual is different and needs to be treated as such, and is to some extent unpredictable.

The primary purpose of management is to manage individuals. If management is 'creative' it will usually be interesting, stimulating and promote dedication to goals.

Perhaps one crucial question to ask is whether people are born with individual characteristics or skills, and if so, what do we inherit genetically or through the physiology of our parents? Also are people trained or conditioned by their early life and which skills and abilities are provided after birth or through continuing education and training later in life? As far as managers are concerned we return to the old adage that managers are born not made. We have been influenced greatly by all these factors, but perhaps the basic behaviour patterns are there from a very early age, and craft and skills and education knowledge can be acquired throughout one's life even to a relatively old age. Some are better able than others to acquire this knowledge and skill continually.

What management has to do is to be creative in recognizing and selecting persons for the most appropriate tasks or job—in terms of creative ability, skills, development, potential, and human relationships.

If a manager does not recognize appropriate abilities and develop these through training and experience to the highest level possible, then he is not making the best use of his resources, and is failing as an effective manager.

The ability to lead people has with it the ability to relate, confer, develop, motivate and be trusted, together with impeccable truthfulness and honesty.

SYSTEMS MANAGEMENT

Many have advocated what is called the 'general systems theory' applied to management. A system is defined by some as an 'organized or complex whole or an assemblage or combination of parts forming a complex unitary whole'. This certainly needs explanation for a more complete understanding. We have transportation systems, telephone systems, economic systems. The word 'system' is being used extensively to refer to many facets of our society.

Many systems are 'closed' systems, some of which are viewed generally as mechanistic—clockwork systems, ignition systems, brake systems. A more complex type of closed system, often referred to as the 'feedback' system, is the self-regulating type such as with thermostatic controls, industrial process controls, and the 'environmental' systems for temperature, humidity and air particle control. The other classes of systems are called 'open' systems, which are often defined as self-maintaining structures, ranging from the cell as the most elementary of these, to genetic societal systems typified by the plant, vegetable, flower or tree, and thence to the animal system with increased mobility, teleological behaviour and self-awareness, and finally to the human level with the ability to use complex language, to communicate, think and remember, and to visualize 'symbolically'. The social system (or systems) of human organization comes next, which includes all forms of cultural systems. The ultimate and absolute are then classified as transcendental systems.

One of the main points of any writing or philosophy of thought is to ask oneself what are the basic assumptions implied. Perhaps within systems is that of *laissez faire*, somehow the system will take care of itself—which is a very dangerous assumption. Any organization or system needs good leadership. Without leadership, an organization will deteriorate; with poor leadership it can also deteriorate very quickly.

DEVELOPING MANAGEMENT SKILLS

A list of the main factors contributing to the development of management skills is given below. More detailed discussion will not be attempted in this overview, as a complete book could be written on the subjects below.

1. Communications.
2. Leadership skills.
3. Teamwork.
4. Decision making.
5. Delegation.
6. Motivating.
7. Improving personal relationships.
8. Counselling/coaching.
9. Time management.

1.3   General analysis of responsibilities

It is very true to say that there is a surprising lack of comprehension in boardrooms regarding the true scope of the production management function, and it is with this in mind, that in general terms a job specification for the production executive is set out. The production executive's task of directing and conducting the manufacturing activities of the company involves the policy function of formulating an overall production strategy, establishing manufacturing priorities and determining the time-scale, all within the broad limits of money, manpower and resources generally, laid down by the board of directors; it also involves the management function of creating the working environment and conditions necessary to achieve the optimum usage of all available resources in terms of men, methods and materials. The scope of production management is thus very wide indeed and calls for a blend of art and science.

Specifically, the production manager must be competent in the following advisory, consultative and executive functions.

1. Advising the board of directors on such matters as:
   (a) availability and potential utilization of manufacturing facilities;
   (b) long-term programmes of manufacturing (in consultation with sales and finance);
   (c) the condition and efficiency of the company's manufacturing equipment (recommendations for disposals, renewals and additions).

2. Consulting with the management of other functions on:
   (a) a budget of optimum range and volume of manufacturing;
   (b) the determination of levels for process work and finished products;
   (c) the determination of manufacturing specifications and standards and the provision of competent staff and adequate facilities, on the basis of information supplied regarding material specifications, quality standards, etc.;
   (d) the provision of inspection facilities for in-process and finished products in accordance with approved procedures and advising and assisting the quality department on the formulation of inspection techniques and procedures.
   (e) the interpretation of standards;
   (f) the provision of research and development facilities;
   (g) preparing and maintaining training and development programmes;
   (h) formulating and maintaining a code of safe practice;
   (i) determining wage rates and supplementary payments;
   (j) compiling a budget of expenditure for manufacturing activities;
   (k) computerized methods and procedures and production systems analysis.

3. Personally ensuring that:
   (a) adequate co-ordination is maintained between production and sales;
   (b) sound planning and control techniques are established;
   (c) there is adequate supervision of production activities;
   (d) suitable programmes are drawn up for planned maintenance of plant and equipment;
   (e) production controllers and supervisors are fully conversant with specifications and standards;

(f)   competent staff and facilities are available for determining manufacturing methods and equipment;

(g)   periodic reviews of finished products are made to ensure conformity with specifications and standards;

(h)   manufacturing difficulties in regard to the interpretation of standards or conformity therewith are taken up with the design department;

(i)   there is a continuous review of the company's manufacturing operations and methods in all their aspects to ensure the maintenance of a high level of effectiveness;

(j)   supervision is motivated to take an enthusiastic interest in the promotion of efficient operating methods;

(k)   suitable procedures for the effective prevention of waste (materials, tools, etc.) are established and enforced;

(l)   plans and provisions are made for the design and manufacture of tools, jigs, fixtures and gauges (including sub-contracted provisions) for the manufacturing programme;

(m)   suitable arrangements are made for the loading of new components or products on specific production centres in accordance with the requirements of overall effectiveness and economy;

(n)   senior personnel in the production section are reasonably up to date with current developments in manufacturing methods, equipment and materials relevant to the company's range of products;

(o)   the purchasing and stock control managers have adequate information and guidance, with particular reference to advance information about production programmes, to facilitate forward ordering, economical purchasing and reliable deliveries, and to provide for the co-ordination of the purchase and delivery of raw materials and tools with the progress of manufacture;

(p)   suitable facilities are available for official visits of factory inspectors and for periodic visits of the company's safety officer;

(q)   statutory and other legal records in respect of manufacturing activities are properly maintained and that all legal requirements are complied with;

(r)   where appropriate, the manufacturing sector is represented in negotiations, e.g., with trade union representatives, dealing with matters of policy affecting the company's employment conditions

11

(as distinct from matters of routine procedure or local disputes) and at meetings concerned with manufacturing methods, e.g., trade association meetings;

(s) adequate steps are taken to maintain, among production supervisors, a genuine interest in the morale and efficiency of shop floor operatives and in the effectiveness of consultation arrangements;

(t) continuous and effective control over the cost of manufacturing operations is maintained;

(u) adequate provision is made for the security and safe custody of that part of the company's property which lies within the production manager's jurisdiction;

(v) policy and interpretation of policy is effectively communicated to functional and line executives and supervisors in such a way as to promote wholehearted participation in the activities and objectives of the company;

(w) responsibilities of functional and line executives and supervisors are known to them and that a sound organizational structure is set up;

(x) production executives and supervisors maintain effective co-operation with the factory services department in regard to standards of maintenance of premises, plant and equipment and for economy in fuel and power.

1.4   Industrial engineering—the key

Effectiveness in operations demands that productivity of all resources is at a high level, particularly when competing within the world market. Perhaps the key role in increasing this productivity lies with the function of industrial engineering.

The American Institute of Industrial Engineering has defined industrial engineering as:

Concerned with the design, improvement and installation of integrated systems of men, materials and equipment. It draws upon specialized knowledge and skill in mathematical, physical and social sciences together with the principles of engineering analysis and design to specify, predict and evaluate the result to be obtained from such systems.

Others have redefined industrial engineering as:

The profession which has the prime objective of making companies more competitive.

12

What is industrial engineering? Perhaps a list of common disciplines would be a useful starter.

1. The layout of factories and design of work flows.
2. Operation methods analysis and design.
3. Work measurement systems.
4. Production and materials control systems.
5. Computer-aided design/computer-aided manufacture (CAD/CAM).
6. Robotics.
7. Production engineering.
8. Cost evaluation and control.

What makes an industrial engineer different to other management specialists?

1. He has the necessary theoretical training in the disciplines involved.
2. He has experience in applying these disciplines in real life working situations.
3. He is trained to implement successfully.
4. He has the necessary time to spend on the project in hand; the manager is too involved in all the day-to-day running of the function for which he is responsible.
5. He must keep up to date and, being a member of a professional institute, promote industrial engineering.

Industrial engineering is based primarily on advances in knowledge, which is generally the source of productivity growth. It has been concluded that 'advances in knowledge is the biggest and most basic reason for the persistent long-term growth of output per unit of input'. The term 'advances in knowledge' must be considered comprehensively. It includes what is usually defined as technical knowledge—concerning physical properties of things and how to make, continue or use them in a physical sense. It also includes 'managerial knowledge'—knowledge of business organization and of managerial techniques considered in the broadest sense. 'Advances in knowledge' comprises knowledge origination in this country and abroad, and knowledge obtained in any way; by organized research, by individual research and by simple observation and experience.

PRODUCTIVITY

Productivity measurement has been studied over many years in order to gain greater insight into what it means. Most recognize that the wealth

13

generation of individual companies, and indeed of nations, depends upon high levels of productivity. In simple terms it means making the best use of our resources. The ratio below provides a measure of productivity:

$$\text{Productivity} = \frac{\text{output}}{\text{input}}$$

The term 'productivity', however, can be applied at different levels, depending upon the viewpoint. This is what makes productivity measurement difficult. At national level, for instance, one often sees indices of gross national product (GNP) *per capita* or per number of people in employment. Within the company it is normally the productivity of labour that is measured.

There are measures we can choose for productivity of capital, perhaps the most usual is 'profit return on net assets employed'. The productivity of materials could be considered to be:

Materials productivity = utilization index × yield × scrap index

Perhaps the biggest problem in a company is to measure overall productivity. Some have suggested the value added approach where:

$$\text{Overall productivity} = \frac{\text{net sales invoiced} - \text{purchased content of sales}}{\text{cost of wages and salaries}}$$

This certainly is one measure of productivity which a few companies use.

H. B. Maynard, an internationally acclaimed firm in the field of provision of precise measurements of productivity, because of its work measurement systems, has defined labour productivity as a combination of three factors:

Labour productivity = methods index × utilization × operator performance

Where *methods index* is the ratio of the work content of the current method being used, divided by the work content of the current best method for the industry concerned.

This is not an easy index to define, but it certainly has a big effect on labour productivity. If, by method changes, the work content can be reduced from eight minutes per piece produced to six minutes per piece produced, but the system has not yet been installed, then the methods index is:

$$\tfrac{6}{8} \times 100 = 75$$

The basis for the ratio will change over time, someone else may look at the same job and reduce the time per piece to three minutes, using a more automated process.

Utilization

is defined by the following furmula:

$$\text{Utilization} = \frac{\text{attendance time} - \text{lost time}}{\text{attendance time}}$$

It is the ratio of the amount of time worked divided by the time available to work. Generally this is influenced by manufacturing support service and management supervision. It can be improved by:

1. Having fewer breakdowns of equipment (maintenance).
2. Planning work more thoroughly (production planning).
3. Fewer shortages of materials (materials management).
4. Organizing people for effective working (production management and supervision).
5. Having less scrap and rectification (quality assurance and control).

Performance

Performance of any person or machine can be achieved only by 'measuring' the work involved. This is normally experienced in standard minutes (SMs) or standard hours (SHs) of expected work—the performance measure is expressed as follows:

$$\frac{\text{Output in SHs (SMs)}}{\text{Time spent on measured work (hours or minutes)}} \times 100$$

PRODUCTIVITY CENTRES

There has, in the last decade, been a rapid development of productivity centres throughout the world, focusing attention on three main aspects of productivity:

1. It is frequently used to describe the health of an economic unit, usually of a country. A large number of studies have been made *comparing* various economic and statistical indices, which purport to indicate something about productivity.
2. Productivity improvement is often recognized as a way to stimulate future business and therefore the wealth of a nation.
3. Studies about how to measure productivity in its many aspects, and how to improve this productivity at micro level have been given a great deal of attention.

15

The School of Business Administration at the University of Western Ontario in Canada, has made a survey of productivity institutions, and published the names and addresses of these in a booklet entitled *Western Productivity Study*. 'Western' refers to the university name and does not mean it is limited to the Western nations. Centres from the Eastern bloc and Asian nations together with the developing nations are also included, making it a world study.

As far as the United Kingdom is concerned, there is no national centre for productivity, although there are a few institutes concerned with certain aspects of it.

The *Western Productivity Study* provides the following numbers of organizations, not all of which are productivity centres:

Africa	17
Asia	28
Australia and New Zealand	6
Western Europe (continent)	57
Eastern Europe	18
Middle East	7
North America	132
United Kingdom	13 (no productivity centres)

Productivity is recognized as a key to future success in the United States, and so there are a great number of centres. They have various names, such as:

- Productivity Centre
- Quality of Working Life Centre
- Productivity Institute
- Quality of Working Life Program
- Office of Productivity Programs.

Many of the developing nations have national productivity boards and centres, often set up with the aid of the United Nations Economic Development Organization and these are an integrated part of their industrial life.

These usually work in the following main areas:

1. To promote the impact of productivity to the public and so change attitudes, through PR, advertising, slogans, public displays, broadcasts, etc.

2. To promote research activities into areas for productivity measurement and improvement.

16

3. To promote courses, lectures, seminars, workshops and conferences to provide knowledge of productivity subjects to delegates.

4. To undertake advisory studies and implementation programmes on productivity improvement.

At the present time the main areas of activity that influence productivity are the following, and should be emphasized:

1. *Economic studies* At macro and micro levels, including managerial economics and econometrics and international aspects.

2. *Managerial studies* The management of organizations, the practice of management, management techniques, behavioural sciences, marketing and selling.

3. *Technological studies* The impact of computers and high technology in society, interaction of R & D, product design, value analysis and engineering, factory automation, office automation.

4. *Industrial engineering.*

5. *Industrial relations.*

6. *Cultural aspects of productivity* How philosophy, religion, culture and science impact on productivity, including their impact on what is called an organization's own 'culture'.

INCREASING PRODUCTIVITY

In many parts of the world there will be significant changes as robots and computerized manufacturing systems replace significant numbers of semi-skilled machine operators and unskilled labourers over the next three decades or so. CAM and robotics will reduce the benefit of mass production relative to batch production and thereby reduce the existing pressures towards product standardization and against diversity and change.

Mass production, by its nature, is compatible only with stabilized or standardized products. Once mass production facilities are in play, usually costing many thousands of pounds, their existence is a deterrent to innovation. Typically the future systems will mean that smaller batches of more variation in product design (but proper standards of tolerance, specifications and fixing devices) can be incorporated into the product's character more easily. However, there is still going to be the need for people in many areas of activity, and getting improvements from existing resources will still be of paramount importance. It is significant that this can be achieved with little capital expenditure through a technique called work study, which is a part of Industrial Engineering.

17

WORK STUDY

1. *Work study* A term for those techniques, particularly *method study* and *work measurement*, which are used in the examination of human work in all its contexts and which leads systematically to the investigation of all the factors which affect efficiency and economy of the situation being reviewed, in order to effect improvement.

2. *Method study* The systematic recording and critical examination of existing and proposed ways of doing work, as a means of developing and applying easier and more effective methods and reducing costs.

3. *Work measurement* The application of techniques designed to establish the time for a qualified worker to carry out a specified job at a defined level of performance.

Introduction

Although much has been written about work study there are many variations in the detailed practice of its components. It is important, however, to be precise about its method of operation, because all too often the results expected do not materialize unless the approach is objective, methodical and practical.

Within the context of modern work study, there are recent developments in various techniques which are necessary for the specialist practitioner which, with intensive training and experience, can make a real impact on effective working within any organization. These techniques are outlined later.

Method study

The object of method study is to develop improvements in layout and methods in order to achieve minimum work content for the operations being studied.

Typical of such improvements are:

1. Proper batching of work to avoid excessive changeover time.

2. Organization of material storage, handling and work flow.

3. Organization of plant and workplace layout to eliminate unnecessary walking and movement.

4. Development of methods enabling both hands to be used productively.

5. Development of methods for performing machine operations on more than one process at a time.

6. Development of productivity aids, such as low-cost automation.

7. Design for production so that cost is reduced or eliminated.

The investigational work for method improvement is a systematic application of the scientific method, which involves:

1. Observation and recording of facts.
2. Analysis and classification of facts.
3. Development of possible answers and proving them by experiment.

The procedure for work study follows a defined sequence:

Select the work or job to be studied.
Record the work through charting and measurement techniques.
Examine the results of the analysis, e.g., critical examination.
Develop new improved methods.
Install, i.e., implement these.
Maintain, i.e., monitor, review and ensure that the results continue.

Process charting

The recording of facts is undertaken in a systematic manner, in which a sequence of events is portrayed diagrammatically by means of a set of process chart symbols to help a person visualize a process as a means of examining and improving it.

Flow charts can be:

1. Man type—what the worker does.
2. Material type—what happens to the material.
3. Equipment type—which records how the equipment is used.

There are many other types of charts used in work study, such as outline process charts, two-handed process charts, multiple activity charts, etc.

Charting symbols (OTIDS)

○	Operation	Indicates the main steps in a process, method or procedure.
⇨	Transport	Indicates the movement of workers, materials or equipment from place to place.
☐	Inspection	Indicates an inspection for quality and/or check for quantity.

19

Delay Indicates a delay in the sequence of events. For example, work waiting between consecutive operations or any object laid aside temporarily without record until required.

Storage Indicates a controlled storage in which a material is received into or issued from stores under some form of authorization, or an item is retained for reference purposes.

DIAGRAMS INDICATING MOVEMENT

Flow diagram

A diagram or model, substantially to scale, which shows the location of specific activities carried out and routes followed by workers, materials or equipment in their execution.

String diagram

One in which a thread is used to trace and measure the routes.

For layout purposes, a modern technique called 'production flow analysis' (PFA) is used to analyse the flow patterns so that groups of work can be linked together.

EXAMINATION

Questioning technique　The means by which the critical examinations are conducted, each activity being subjected in turn to a systematic and progressive series of questions (see Fig. 1.1).

Creative thinking　A philosophy based on psychological principles which examines the way in which creative thinking takes place—and uses those aspects to bring about improved methods.

PRINCIPLES OF MOTION ECONOMY

Minimum movements　Movements which, while natural, are the minimum needed for the job.

Simultaneous movements　Movements in which different limbs are working at the same time.

Symmetrical movements　Movements which are so arranged that they can be performed on the right and left sides of the body about an imaginary line through the centre of the body.

20

Element description... DATE ....
Reference ....

Present facts	Is it necessary?	Alternatives	Selected alternative for development
Purpose What is achieved?	If yes—why?	Yes No What else could be done?	What?
Place Where is it done?	Why there?	Where else could it be done?	Where?
Sequence When is it done?	Why then?	When else could it be done?	When?
Person Who does it?	Why that person?	Who else could do it?	Who?
Means How is it done? (Method)	Why that way?	How else could it be done?	How?

Fig. 1.1 Critical examination sheet

Natural movements   Movements which make the best use of the shape and arrangement of the parts of the body involved.

Rhythmical movements   A sequence of movements which induces a natural rhythm when repeated.

Habitual movements   Movements designed, through precise repetition, to become a habit.

Continuous movements   Movements which are smooth and curved and which avoid sharp changes of direction.

In modern practice, the techniques of predetermined motion time system (PMTS) are increasingly used to reduce movements (see 'Techniques of work measurement', page 23).

WORK MEASUREMENT

The object of work measurement is to obtain a standard time for performing a task. It is expressed in standard minutes (SMs) or standard hours (SHs), and is set on the following basis:

1.   A defined method is normally laid down in a document called a production method standard (PMS).
2.   By a qualified operator, i.e., one who is skilled and proficient at the task.
3.   At a specified performance, i.e., the rate of output at which the worker performs over the working day at a specified efficiency level.
4.   Inclusive of contingency and rest allowances. These are allowances for occasional elements of work which are non-repetitive, allowances for personal needs and to overcome fatigue.

Time standards are needed:

1.   To make predictions of accurate delivery dates.
2.   To load machines, processes and manual sections to produce the best use of available resources.
3.   To make it possible to cost each item of work realistically.
4.   To provide facts on which sales potential can be compared against budget.
5.   To provide realistic estimates for new work.

Higher productivity provides opportunities for raising the general standard of living:

22

1. Larger supplies of both consumer goods and capital goods at lower costs and higher prices.
2. Higher real earnings.
3. Improvement in working conditions.
4. A strengthening of the foundation of human well-being.

Do not forget the human factor in work study—we are dealing with individuals and are all different and react in different ways.

TECHNIQUES OF WORK MEASUREMENT

These are:

Time study
Activity sampling
Synthetics
Predetermined motion time system (PMTS)
Analytical estimating
Comparative estimating
Multiple regression analysis (MRA)
Computerized planning and estimating

STANDARD PERFORMANCE

Standard performance is the rate of output which qualified workers will naturally achieve without over-exertion, as an average over the working day or shift, provided they know, and adhere to, the specified method, and provided they are motivated to apply themselves to their work. It is recommended that this is denoted by 100 on the British scale, corresponding to the production of 1 standard hour (SH) or 60 standard minutes (SM) of work in 60 minutes.

TAKING TIME STUDIES

In order to take a time study of operations, the first requirement is to break down each job into small elements of work, each of which takes a time in the range of 6 to 30 seconds. A list of these elements in sequence provides a complete description of the job and would be obtained from a complete method study of each operation.

Each of these elements is timed separately on a fly-back type stopwatch, and for each time recorded, the Studyman's assessment of speed and effectiveness with which the element was performed.

This assessment is expressed numerically on a rating scale known as the British Standards Institution (BSI) scale. A rating of 100 means that the operator is working at that speed which, with an appropriate allowance for rest, would result in the production of 60 SMs of work in an hour. This is the average expected under good conditions or incentives.

WORKING UP THE TIME STUDY

Each element of time recorded is multiplied by the assessment given and the product divided by 100. This produces a basic time which is the actual time required to perform the element at a performance equal to 100 rating, e.g.:

22 actual seconds $\times$ 90 assessment $\div$ 100 = 20 basic seconds

25 actual seconds $\times$ 80 assessment $\div$ 100 = 20 basic seconds

18 actual seconds $\times$ 110 assessment $\div$ 100 = 20 basic seconds

In this way, the varying pace at which work is performed can be taken into account and a constant basic time per element is established. The resulting basic time for each element (plus contingencies and occasional elements) in the study is then entered on a study summary sheet.

THE SET-UP

In the majority of cases it is not desirable to rely on a single study for establishing an SM value. An analysis and comparison of several studies will be required and a study analysis sheet is prepared in the same manner as a study summary sheet but with provision for recording data from several studies on one sheet.

In the simplest case, where identical products are being manufactured, the study analysis sheet can be completed by taking an arithmetical mean of the basic time for the operation.

In other cases, where the work is of the processing type, successive studies may be on a different size or shape of material. In such cases the individual element times of the analysis sheet are used to determine the relationship of the recorded basic element times to the governing factor of size, etc. This can be portrayed on a graph showing the relationship, for instance, of weight against time. This is used for the derivation of what is called 'synthetics'.

THE STANDARD TIME

The object of work measurement is to obtain the work content of an operation or task. The methods used to achieve this have changed significantly over the past few years, although the components of a 'standard' time have remained constant in outline.

Basic work content

The time actually to perform the operation or task at a defined level of performance. The universally recognized basis is the methods time management (MTM) method of establishing standard data, which is the most consistent and reliable of all the methods.

The British standard for basic work content called basic minutes or basic hours, is evaluated at 1.2 × MTM. When time study is used a technique called 'rating' is used to convert actual minutes observed to basic minutes of work content.

Contingency allowance

This is normally a small percentage allowance on the basic work content, to allow for infrequent work which is normally carried out, but which has not been allowed in the basic work content. This allowance should always be established by actual observations over a period of time, and would be different for each organization and type of task.

Relaxation allowance

This is a further percentage for two different requirements:

1. *Personal needs* This normally includes allowances for going to the lavatory, for ten minutes' refreshment each morning and each afternoon, and any stoppages which occur throughout the working day of less than two minutes' duration. The refreshment breaks need not be specified periods, but could be taken at any time depending on the local agreement.

2. *Fatigue allowances* These are relaxation allowances to overcome physiological fatigue because of special needs of the task in hand, for example, working in a hot atmosphere or constantly lifting weights. Many of these factors ought to be designed out of the task. Most practitioners would use tables prepared by the International Labour Organization (ILO) for this purpose, although many countries have published their own standards for this component.

When the three components of standard time, described above, are added together, the result is usually described as the standard time and in British standard terminology, is stated as standard minutes (SM) and standard hours (SH). Any allowances in addition to the above, should not be described as standard time. A bad practice often used in industry is to increase the standard time by a policy allowance; such a standard should be called an 'allowed time' and not a 'standard time'.

25

PREDETERMINED MOTION TIME SYSTEMS

A work measurement technique whereby times established for the human motions (classified according to the nature of the motion and conditions under which it is made) are used to build up the time for a job at a defined level of performance.

The first generation of these techniques was very detailed and the basic movements were broken into very minute motion patterns (MTM-1, work factor).

In the second generation, it was found that in many applications the small motion patterns were continually being repeated giving rise to synthesized data for broader elements. For instance, in MTM-2, single basic MTM motions were derived which were combinations of MTM-1 motions.

The advantages of MTM-2 are:

1. Consistency between analysts.

2. Fast to handle.

3. Universally named.

4. Easy to understand.

5. Descriptive of the method.

6. Combinable with other MTM data.

7. Specified in relation to speed of accuracy and accuracy of results.

MTM-2 is intended for operations longer than 0.75 minutes, with an accuracy of ±5 per cent at time cycles of a single minute. It is usually reckoned to be four times faster to apply than MTM-1.

MTM-3, which uses larger groups of motions than MTM-2, was developed in Sweden, particularly for maintenance and non-repetitive work. It provides a 95 per cent confidence level of ±5 per cent accuracy at time cycles of 10 minutes' duration and ±10 per cent accuracy at time cycles of 2.5 minutes' duration. It is reckoned to be three times faster to apply than MTM-2.

Other developments used in Britain include tape data analysis (TDA), tape data and data block approach. PMTS systems have been developed particularly for specific applications:

– UMS (universal maintenance standards)
– CWD (clerical work data)

26

THIRD GENERATION TECHNIQUES

The most recently developed technique of PMTS is MOST (Maynard Operation Sequence Technique), which allocates a series of times for a whole sequence of motions.

MOST is based on what are called 'sequence models' for different kinds of manual activity. Examples are given in Table 1.1.

Table 1.1 Sequence models for manual activities

Activity	Sequence model	Sub-activities
General move	ABGABPA	A—action distance B—body motion G—gain control P—place
Controlled move	ABGMXIA	M—move controlled X—process time I—align
Tool use	ABGABP ABPA	F—fasten L—loosen M—measure R—record S—surface treat T—think

In addition to the classes in Table 1.1 there are also categories for heavy work involving:

1. Move with jib crane.
2. Move with bridge crane.
3. Move with wheeled truck (manual and powered).

METHODS OF DETERMINING THE BASIC WORK CONTENT

There are many different methods in use for determining the work content of a task. The greatest need is to establish a fast but reliable method for work measurement in the following ways:

Accuracy
Consistency
Simple data development
Economy
Ease of use and updating
Methods orientation

THE NEED FOR ACCURACY

Four factors contribute to the accuracy of work measurement:

The level of accuracy desired

This is normally considered by practitioners to be ± 5 per cent.

The balancing time

This is the period over which the desired level of accuracy must be attained. Eight hours? Forty hours?

The balancing effect is defined as 'the levelling out of individual deviations for a smaller total deviation'. Table 1.2 gives the balancing time for MTM-based systems.

Table 1.2   Balancing time for MTM-based systems

Work measurement technique	Balancing time	
	(TMUs)	(Seconds)
MTM-1	600	21.6
MTM-2	1 600	57.6
MOST	3 200	115.2
MTM-3	15 000	540.0

Degree of repetitiveness of activity

If a job repeats itself frequently, there needs to be a greater consistency of the value—measured by deviation of mean value and by standard deviation of scatter of the values. If the same job only repeats itself occasionally, such as with maintenance work, then the operator will not have time for the learning curve to take effect.

The duration of the activity being considered

If the proportion of the total working time of an activity is high, then there is a need for greater accuracy. The spread of values for a short cycle assembly job should be much less than for a maintenance job, where the total allowable deviation should be greater—sometimes a maintenance job will go very easily and at other times the same job will have stiff bolts or bearings which have seized hard.

The theory of added variances is one that can adequately cover these four factors, given by

$$r_t = R_T \sqrt{\frac{T}{n \times t}}$$

where:

r_t = the measured activity's allowed deviation in per cent.
R_T = the required total allowed deviation in per cent.
T = the total time (balancing time) in hours.
n = the activity's occurrence frequency in T.
t = the activity's measured time in hours.

Tables have been designed to take into account each of these factors when applying standard times. One of the faults that is common with many practitioners is that they often set standards with more implied precision than is the actual case.

THE NEED FOR CONSISTENCY

Many techniques of work measurement are prone to analyst errors. This is particularly true of the more detailed PMTS systems such as MTM-1, it is also true of time study.

Attempts have been made to reduce inconsistencies through the use of synthetics and data bases of elemental times, or through rating clinics; but it is still surprising how varied are the results of work measurement programmes within companies.

The new techniques such as MOST and Computerized work measurement are much better in the respect of consistency.

THE NEED FOR SIMPLE DATA DEVELOPMENT

The third generation of work measurement techniques such as MOST offers this simplicity of application. Numerous comparison studies have shown that it is as accurate as other, far more complicated, systems.

In terms of compactness, the more detailed the analysis that is necessary, the greater the number of pages of documentation, and the greater the amount of practitioner skills that are needed to maintain consistency. Table 1.3 is typical of some PMTS techniques.

Table 1.3 Assembly of a carburettor as an example of PMTS techniques

Work measurement technique	No. of pages of documentation	Standard time (TMUs)
MTM-1	16	4402
MTM-2	10	4446
MTM-3	8	4950
MOST	1	4530
Time study	4	varied

THE NEED FOR ECONOMY

The latest techniques—computerized systems or MOST—are much faster to apply than the older techniques such as time study. In terms of PMTS Table 1.4 gives an indication of application speed and hence costs. MOST is considered to be at least three times as fast as time study to apply.

Table 1.4   Application speed and costs in terms of PMTS

Work measurement technique	Total of TMUs assigned per analyst hour
MTM-1	300
MTM-2	1 000
MTM-3	3 000
MOST	12 000

As far as computerized work measurement systems are concerned, they will depend on the application considered. Generally they are faster to apply—needing only an applicator rather than a standards development analyst.

The main economy of computerized systems is that they can combine standards application, process planning, cost estimating and typing of documents together. Some companies claim that computerized systems take between 10 and 15 per cent of the total time for the equivalent manual systems.

THE NEED FOR EASE OF USE AND UPDATING

One of the problems with time study is that methods can change, without the analyst being aware that anything has happened—only that the times are getting loose. This may be because of incorrect application in the first place, and the learning curve effect has taken place to loosen times. It may be that genuine method changes have been effected, but elemental times and descriptions are inadequate to spot the difference.

Two separate problems exist alongside this:

1. Wage drift is a common occurrence.

2. Maintaining accurate time standards is also very difficult, because of shop floor and union attitudes prevalent in the United Kingdom.

Any system of work measurement in use should be easily updated, and should be readily understood in principle by operatives, so that they are convinced of the fairness and consistency of the results.

Table 1.5 shows examples of MOST techniques. There are different versions of MOST, now a complete system of work measurement which has

Table 1.5 MOST techniques

Technique	Index base	Applied to	Previous technique
Mini MOST	1	Short cycle operations	MTM-1
MOST	10	Ordinary operations	MTM-2 Time study
Maxi MOST	100	Non-repetitive work, e.g., maintenance	MTM-3 UMS
Clerical MOST	10	Clerical operations	MTM-C

virtually rendered MTM and time study obsolete in terms of applicability, though not in terms of practice. The United Kingdom has been very slow to adapt to this method as yet, although it has been used in Sweden, the United States, Western Europe and even in the Eastern Bloc, e.g., Hungary.

COMPUTERIZED SYSTEMS OF ESTIMATING, PLANNING AND STANDARD DATA

These are systems of data building based on computerized programs, and storage of basic data in disk files. It is usual to link the systems together into a chain of activities combining methods engineering, process planning and selection of process time variables (such as for machine shops, sewing machines or chemical plant variables). Part data can be built up into various levels of precision and application (Table 1.6).

Table 1.6 Part data build-up

Level	Examples
3rd	For estimating and pre-planning (fairly coarse data)
2nd	For factory loading, production planning. Group bonus scheme (combining averages of data, etc.)
1st	Elemental time standards or for individual incentive scheme (based on MTM-2 or time standards)
Elementary	Back up data—elementary MTM-1 patterns and minute process time data

As the nature of the data approaches a higher level so the precision becomes less, but the application time becomes faster.

Generally, most computer systems are built up from the company's own data bank and can incorporate MTM-2 patterns, speeds and feeds, time study synthetics, etc., but a few are based on the supplier's own data and on

31

the principles of time slotting, and statistical methods of frequency allocation for the highests occurring repetitive or partitions of these.

There are generally two types of computer systems applicable:

1. The minicomputer with hard disks, with two or more screens and printers and costing about £15 000 +.

2. The microcomputer with floppy disks, screen and printer and costing about £3000.

Examples of these systems are:

1. LOCAM available from Logan Associates Ltd and P-E Consulting Ltd, based on DEC(PDP11/34) or DG(Nova or Eclipse) minicomputers or mainframes.

   Output examples:
   Process time masters for detailed machine operation sequences.
   Time computation sheet—element times for each process element.
   Manufacturing instructions—process planning sheet showing sequences of operations, times, machines, etc.

   Data base:
   Patterns—small elements and time.
   Tables—matrix of times related to variables.
   Macros—logical associations of elements.

2. CAPES and SUPERCAPES available from Methods Workshop, and Inbucon Productivity Services Ltd, based on micro- or minicomputers.

   Output examples:
   Process time masters.
   Time computation sheets.
   Manufacturing instructions.
   Available for light, medium and heavy machine shops, tool rooms, press work, fabrication and assembly data.

3. SOFIE 2   This system is similar to CAPES and has been developed by Organisation Development Ltd.

4. CEEQUEL   Another similar system offered from Scott Grant Ltd.

5. REAP-3 available from P-E Consulting Ltd, based on microcomputers or programmable calculator.

   Output examples:
   Time values or estimates.

   Data base:
   Statistical indexed time value and code evaluation.

6. REACT available from P-E Consulting Ltd, based on microcomputer (single or multi-user).

   Output examples:
   Material list and assembly listing.
   Component routing information.
   Estimating routines.
   Made in/brought out index.
   Shop loading and cost files.

   Data base:
   Simplified data for estimating purposes.

7. MOST—computer available from H. B. Maynard & Co Ltd, based on minicomputer.

   Output examples:
   Work place layout.
   Method description/feeds and speeds.
   Allocation of manual and process time.

   Data base:
   Synthetic values for process time, and MOST operation sequence elements. It is possible to incorporate a line balancing program into this system.

   As is generally the case with most computerized systems, it is the larger company which has made the first installations, but as time progresses medium-sized companies will also be implementing such systems.

8. TEL Some computerized systems of time study and activity sampling have been developed by Telford Management Services Ltd—the name prefixed by TEL, e.g., TELTIME.

NEED FOR METHODS ORIENTATION

One of the biggest drawbacks with time study is that being based on 'element descriptions', there is very limited methods orientation. With MTM systems, by designing the method, one is automatically obtaining the time. Time and method are related—if you walk twice as far it takes double the time, if you pick up an item from twice the distance it takes double the time, and so on. The effect of method on time is directly seen with PMTS, but this is not so with time study.

TIME MANAGEMENT

The management of time is of vital necessity, as much for the managing director as for the office worker and the manufacturing operator. Do we each use our time to the maximum possible benefit to the company?

For manufacturing control, time is the basic building block for any proper assessment of effectiveness. Without proper time management, we are building our factory on the sand.

Proper time standards are needed:

1. To predict accurate delivery dates.
2. To load machines, processes and manual sections, so that balanced workloads are possible.
3. To plan and sequence work programmes.
4. To obtain consistent cost records, and to predetermine standard costs.
5. As a basis for flexible budgeting.
6. To provide an accurate basis for calculating financial benefits and costs savings.

It is important that time is separated from incentive payment; many problems in industry have resulted because this principle is not recognized.

Time is often changed to enable operators to receive additional compensation. This should *never* be allowed to happen. If taken to its logical extreme, it is absurd that five minutes (which is factual) is allowed to become 7 minutes (which is a distortion of the truth). Time is a scientifically verifiable measure. The rate per time at which payment is made is variable and negotiable—adjustments to wage payments would always be made through wage rates, and not by altering an unalterable, which time is.

CONCLUSION

Work study is a foundation technique for modern production management. In addition to helping to achieve maximum productivity of resources of manpower, capital and plant, it provides basic data for ascertainment and control of labour costs through modern techniques of costing.

It enables balanced production programmes to be applied to achieve optimum utilization of labour and machines, subject to the limitations imposed by availability of materials and the order book position.

PRODUCTIVITY THE KEY

Without productivity objectives a business does not have direction. Without productivity measurement, it does not have control.

2

Forecasting and production planning

Chapter 2 is concerned with the first of the three principal problem areas of production management, namely forecasting and production planning. The need to establish realistic short-term and medium-term forecasts of product demand and its implications for resource requirements is essential for all planning and control decisions that follow from it. It is therefore important that all production managers are at least aware of the scope and the function of a range of statistical and other forecasting techniques which would be appropriate in their own environment. Section 2.1 looks into the range of techniques that could be used for demand forecasting. Having established realistic forecasts of product demand, the next stage in the planning process is that of relating the entire demand pattern to available capacity so that overall plans and targets can be set for all of the operations involved. This task—aggregate and capacity planning—is described in Sec. 2.1 along with the issues involved in the choice of appropriate strategies for it. The process of developing the production plan in terms of matching demand patterns with available resources is briefly described (Sec. 2.3). Also included in this Chapter (Sec. 2.4) is the often discussed topic of 'batching of work' especially some of the practical consequences of using economical batch quantities (EBQ).

2.1 Demand forecasting

Everyone makes forecasts, from schoolchildren selecting their A-levels to the small businessman who has just started trading, to the Prime Minister of the United Kingdom. Many will state that this is not forecasting but prediction; others will feel we are 'star gazing' or perhaps looking into a

35

crystal ball. We are all making some assessment of what is likely to happen based on some assumptions.

The small businessman has started his operations with an optimism about the goods or services he is offering. On the basis of this optimism, he is prepared to spend a given amount of money and to work hard to succeed in the areas of opportunity he has 'spotted'. His assumptions may be good or may be ill-founded. In starting off in an operation there may be very little factual data which would confirm his impressions and feelings. Perhaps some acquaintances have responded 'positively' thinking that his ideas are good ones; or more likely he has some knowledge of social or technical trends which he would like to exploit in a way which would be beneficial for both society and himself.

Incidentally, an assumption wrongly established is called a presumption!

The Prime Minister making assessments of the economy is dealing with something that is extremely complex.

Forecasts of likely future events are made by economists, usually by what are called economic models. This is a computerized simulation of the major economic trends which are thought to have an impact on a country's economic well-being. Many of the relationships between the cause and the effect have been made by computerized statistical significance and correlation tests, so that the likelihood of making errors is reduced. This science is called 'econometrics', but it still results in presumption by the political decision makers. The Prime Minister and the Cabinet colleagues are not usually professional economists; they rely heavily on trained staff in the Treasury and on economic advisers; and they all often get it wrong!

What chance then has the business got in making what are called demand forecasts! Fortunately the business market, although complex, is not fraught with so many difficulties as the political arena. Most established companies also have a record of history from which to draw—not that historical data are necessarily a preview of future events, for this would be far from true—having measurable data does assist in understanding a situation, and can be useful in predicting what may happen in the future.

Whether the management of a company is dreaming up a forecast off the top of its head, or making an assumption on the back of a cigarette packet, it is making some prediction of the future. It is much better sense to use available business data in order to do two main things:

1. To gain an understanding of what is happening. The scientists have gained a much better appreciation of the world we live in by using measurements and following what is called the 'scientific method'. The tendency now is to think our knowledge adequate when this is far from being the case.

2. To give a higher reliability and accuracy to our predictions. Reliability in simple terminology is the percentage of times our prediction is adequate in terms of accuracy. Accuracy means that our forecast is within a given deviation from the actual statistical mean of the result.

Prediction has been studied over many thousands of years—in the ancient Near East the science of astrology was developed to a remarkable extent. In ancient China and India we have read of 'wise men' who developed many philosophical thoughts about the world and its predictions.

In modern times there are many people who will purport to tell us about the future—through almanacs, horoscopes, crystal ball gazing, and other mediumistic channels. These predictions are often derided, but we may harbour thoughts that they may be true. The fact that these methods are sometimes accurate does not belie the fact that they are highly dangerous and are often misrepresentations or slightly devious distortions of the truth.

There is one source that is often correct about future events: this is called prophecy. The problem here is that many claim to be prophets when clearly they are not. Prophets are usually fairly clearly recognized. The main point about these few paragraphs is that statistical forecasting is not the only means of prediction, and it is probably not the best method, but it is the only realistic way for most people. There are many instances when the businessman has steered a course which conflicted with all the evidence, and with all the advice he received from colleagues. He did what he considered to be the 'right thing' and succeeded. Only those with deeply held convictions should try this approach; those who are more uncertain should be prepared to do the following:

1. Get the best factual data available, and try to understand the implications of the 'message'.

2. Seek the best advice possible—good reliable counsel from more than one person is always a sound proposition. It is important to think through any implication and to make up one's own mind eventually—even against advice.

Many will take the 'middle road' approach and end up with mediocrity of result, for fear of being wrong or of being made redundant. Too many people have tried to hide behind detailed market research data or scientific sales forecasts and have not reacted to the real opportunities which a business could command. It is necessary to be brave and wise!

Up to this point, many will feel that demand forecasting has not been covered. Our own answer to this is that far too many people do not see the total situation in which forecasts have to be made, and many regard demand forecasting only as the scientific analysis of data.

In more strict terminology demand forecasting may be distinguished from prediction as follows:

Demand forecasting The statistical treatment of past data to give an estimate of the future demand. In this strict definition market research, opinion polls, and end-use market studies are still past data.

Prediction This involves the use of market intelligence and management instinct for the same purpose.

REASONS FOR FORECASTING

The first question to be asked in demand forecasting is 'For what purpose are the forecasts needed?' All businesses need to make preparations ahead of time. In the first place annual budgets of revenue and expenditure are necessary for profit management purposes, and for the financial needs of the business. Many companies have to purchase raw materials and other stocks in advance of actual orders, and so some forecasting becomes necessary.

The reasons for forecasting can generally be divided into three main classes; these will be called:

Long-term forecasts

Medium-term forecasts

Short-term forecasts

Long-term forecasts

These are defined as demand forecasts extending beyond twelve months and up to five years in advance. The main purpose for this type of forecast is to manage the future direction of the business. The data needed will be:

1. Data about trends and directions of the products—market size and share.
2. Data regarding the effect on the business of economic and socio-technical trends.
3. Data about changes which will affect people's choice about their own market commodity; in this case, sensitivity to price, service, presentation, advertising, method of selling and brand-switching behaviour.

The time base for these forecasts would normally be quarterly or annual periods.

Medium-term forecasts

These are defined as demand forecasts extending beyond three months and up to twelve months ahead. The main purpose for this type of forecast is for the annual operating budgets, cash budgets, overall production plans, and for assessing the bought-out parts and materials which need ordering in advance.

The time base for these forecasts would normally be monthly.

Short-term forecasts

These are defined as forecasts up to three months ahead. The main purpose is to make more sensitive adjustments to the budgeted plans, and in some cases for setting inventory control parameters.

The time base for these would normally be weekly.

SPECIFICITY OF FORECASTING

In making forecasts it is also most important to be specific about what one is forecasting. The definition of what constitutes a market for a particular product is one aspect of this. Each market often needs dividing into particular sectors to provide relevant data. Take, for instance, the total car market. The first question is 'What is defined by a car?' Does it include:

Three wheelers
Invalid carriages
Motorized carriages?

Is it limited to:

Petrol engined vehicles
Saloon cars?

Of more importance is the particular market segment one is attempting to service. If one is selling Rolls Royce, it is clearly different in many respects to selling BL motors.

Market segments can be apportioned by price, range, size of vehicle, engine capacity or by some consumer index on spending power. Which is the most realistic for the purpose in mind?

It is only when the basic questions have been asked that the appropriate mathematical technique can be selected.

In this chapter, the main methods only will be outlined, as a full treatment would necessitate far more complexity and text.

For production control (PC) purposes four main exponents of demand are usually present:

Level of demand
Trend
Seasonal variation
Random fluctuation about basic pattern

Demand

In an analysis of demand for sales management purposes and for PC, it is necessary to have regular computerized statistics for products and product groups which are often divided into:

Market type—defined by end use for product.
Market outlets—defined by how the product is sold to the end user.
Market territory—defined by area in which the product is sold.
Salesman—defined by the company's own salesman concerned.

Practice has also led to asking for display graphs to be made of the actual sales and the trend line of these sales on the same time series.

Any change to the current situation can usually be picked up far more quickly by inspecting the visual graphic display than by looking at tables on a screen or printout.

For planning purposes, however, the statistical value tables are vital.

Trend

This component is normally calculated by two main methods:

1. Moving average.
2. Weighted moving average (exponential smoothing and its variants).

Table 2.1 is often useful in interpreting the approximate relationship between the two methods.

Table 2.1 Relationship between methods used to calculate trend

No. of periods Moving average	Smoothing constant ' '
3	0.5
5	0.33
7	0.25
9	0.2
19	0.1
39	0.05

Seasonality

Three main methods are used to forecast monthly or period variations in demand:

1. *Base series* Demand in a particular month is related to the average demand by multiplying constant.

40

2. *Cumulative series*   Each month the total demand for the year to date is forecast. Actual demand is then compared. A small percentage variation at the start of the season can give evidence of a much greater effect later on.

3. *Sine waves*   These are natural periodical wavelengths, which can be added together or subtracted to simulate potential seasonality.

Forecast errors

This is the unresolved variation of forecasts to actual figures. For calculating safety requirements in terms of spare production capacity or safety stocks for a given service level, a normal distribution is usually assumed, and the variation measured by standard deviation.

OTHER METHODS OF DEMAND FORECASTING

There are many other methods of demand forecasting for which reference to the appropriate textbook should be made. For example:

Gompertz or logarithmic curves for product life history
Single or multiple regression analysis
Input-output analysis
Market research studies
End-use market studies
Marketing modelling techniques

2.2   Production planning

There are different levels of production planning, corresponding to the time horizon of demand forecast and policy established for the company. This is shown in Table 2.2.

Each major function within a company will need its own plan over the different time horizons—marketing, technical, manufacture and finance. Each must, of course, be co-ordinated and linked together so that people are not working at cross-purposes.

Plans should be not only a projection of the past but also a realistic target of achievable performance for the future—improving the present situation and reaching realistic goals of achievement.

2.3   The production plan

The first stage is to translate the desired forecast into the production plan, by checking that the manufacturing plant is able to meet it. This is known as aggregate or capacity planning.

Table 2.2 Production planning

Type of forecast	Plan horizon	Questions to answer
Long term	Strategic plan 5–10 years	What business are we in? Where are we going? What must be done today to prepare for the expected future? Do we need new factories, distribution centres, offices?
Long term	Business plan 2–5 years	What is the total market for each product–market group? What is the market share? Which markets are declining? How fast? Which are stable? Which are gaining? How fast? What new products are needed? Which new market areas need penetrating?
Medium term	Production plan 1–2 years	How well is present plant utilized? Is equipment/tooling adequate? What new technology is to be introduced? Which products need dropping, phasing in? Capital investment decisions within plant?
Short term	Master production schedule $\frac{1}{4}$–1 year	What specific products are to be made? How many? When? What materials/parts are needed? How many? When? What capacity constraints exist? What material constraints exist?

To check a sales forecast against plant capacity, most companies would calculate the capacity needed in terms of direct labour man hours (for assembly) or in terms of machine hours (for process-based activities). The total number of man hours needed would be obtained by multiplying, for each product, the number of labour man hours per week by the number of products required. Then sum up the various products' requests, and get the workload.

Unfortunately, it is necessary to undertake these calculations in a little more detail because there will be a staggering of some of the man hours needed, because of lead times, several weeks or days before the products are finished. The whole basis is to apportion the workloads to the weeks and months in which they will occur. Sometimes it is necessary, because of tight spots in capacity, to limit what can be produced through some key machines. The aggregate planning must be reliable, and be based on the shop performances one is likely to get, therefore one is unlikely to get eight hours of scheduled work out of each eight attendance hours. Holidays and downtime will have to be taken into account.

Some companies use measures other than hours to load this capacity. Some of these are usually too simple to be truly effective, such as total sales in pounds sterling, but there may be other measures which are satisfactory; for instance, loom hours in a textile plant, cars per shift in a vehicle assembly plant, or equivalent standard products (ESP) where there is a group of products with slight variations to each. As a general rule standard hours (SHs) are the best measure for capacity.

Other factors may have to be taken into account at this stage—the availability of significant items of materials making up the product, cash resources available, shortage of plans and skills.

At this stage, it is important not to regard the production as absolutely fixed; some alterations are possible, as are changes in the capacity, e.g., overtime, new employees, number of shifts, etc.

From this capacity plan the overall master production plan is derived, often called the master schedule. The main purpose of this form of planning is to establish what is feasible, and not to take on promises that cannot be met in practice.

THE MASTER PRODUCTION SCHEDULE (MPS)

More detail is needed in the MPS than in the production plan. The production plan will often focus on product groups, or classes of work and will be an annual plan broken into quarters or, more realistically, months. The production plan is an agreed schedule for manufacture which will be different but linked to the marketing plan—if sales demand is seasonal it may be necessary to manufacture for stock at certain times of the year. Sales may fluctuate but manufacture should be steady.

The MPS will focus on individual products or individual parts and materials sold directly to the customer—alternatively, it may focus on standard modules that make up the item sold to the customer. Products or assemblies specified in the MPS must be described by individual bills of materials.

The purpose of MPS is:

1. To integrate the production plans with the day-to-day operations.
2. To form the basis for managerial control within the company—what happens at the MPS stage vitally affects customer service, stocks held, production output and cash flows, so it is very important.
3. To focus on and be the basis for formal, integrated planning and control—of production and of materials.

PRODUCTION PLANNING AND CONTROL—A SYSTEM OVERVIEW

Improved planning and control of manufacturing operations is recognized today as vital to the needs of giving a good customer service, achieving good utilization of equipment and personnel and of having a planned flow of cash. Production planning and control is the area where different departmental objectives are co-ordinated together to achieve the optimum performance for the company.

The basic system for production planning and control is common to all manufacturing companies—but each company will have different detailed applications of the system. This basic system is shown in Fig. 2.1.

2.4 The batching of work

There is much that has been written about batching work and the concept of economical batch quantities (EBQ). The basic assumptions are that the more stock that is held, the greater will be the cost of carrying that stock; and the larger the batch the smaller will be the cost of each individual item (whether purchased or manufactured).

There are two different costs working in opposite directions; there is a high cost of very small batches, and a high cost of very large batches; somewhere in the middle is the point of least cost at a given batch size (the EBQ).

There are important truths expressed by the formulae given for working out the EBQ; however, some of the practical consequences of using the EBQs should be thought out carefully before putting them into practice. The reasons for doing so are mainly in the practicalities of manufacture.

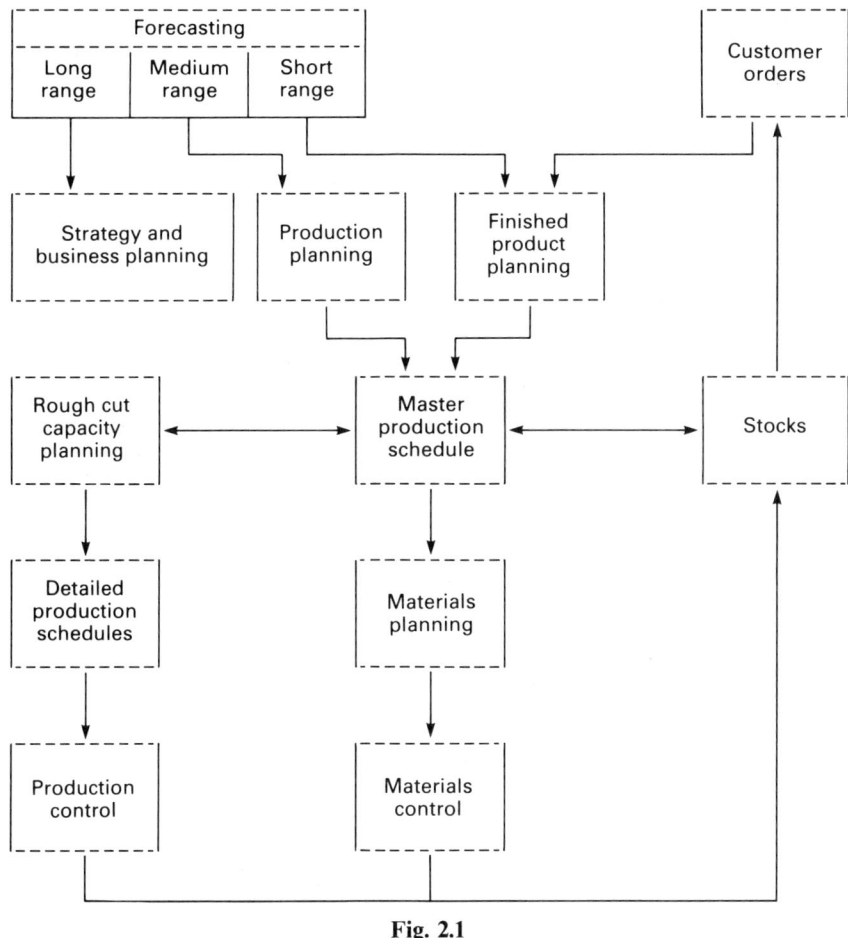

Fig. 2.1

ASSEMBLIES

Assemblies, particularly final assemblies (complete products) are usually costly, easily damaged, can be bulky and of supreme importance, once an item has been used in a final assembly it cannot be used for anything else (except by taking the assembly apart if that is possible). They are also expensive to carry in finished stock.

The basic question that has to be answered from the point of view of production and marketing is 'Do we assemble continuously or do we assemble in lots?' This is a basic question and an important one for each manufacturing (and servicing) operation.

In the first place, the basic consideration is 'Are our demands such that we can make products or parts all the time to meet that demand, in which case, we have to stop making at times?' However, we must first decide what capacity to set up in the manufacturing plant.

We set up the basic resources of manpower, materials, machining and money—in this case for the final assembly arrangements (an assembly line, an assembly area, or an assembly work station, according to the perceived needs of the operation). The final assembly of each product will have very different characteristics. For instance:

1. *Motor cars* Usually high-value consumer-orientated markets necessitating capital intensive assembly lines, where the car body is kept moving from the beginning to the end. Each stage adds something to the assembly (mostly by adding sub-assemblies such as engines, transmission units, wheels, electrical sub-assemblies—lights, dashboard units, etc.). A large percentage of the parts and sub-assemblies are bought from specialists outside the company.

2. *Furniture* Not usually such a high-value market, but extremely customer-orientated.

    Characteristics of batch manufacture of different types/styles of furniture, using either specialist word-working machinery or fabricating the sub-assemblies used (a laminate for instance, is a sub-assembly). Because of alternative types/styles being offered in the market-place the final assembly will normally be completed in batches of work.

3. *Component production (with assembly)* This is *mostly* parts manufacture where *some* assembly takes place (this will be final assembly to the component manufacturers, and sub-assembly to the final assembler).

    Here the final assembly will vary considerably according to the service operated by the company. The particular requirement may be assembled only once, in which case a general-purpose work station will be needed; or there may be regular contracts, in which case the assembly unit could be an assembly line with specialist work stations, using assembly aids where feasible (e.g., pneumatic hand-held equipment, jigged fixtures, vibrating bowl feed mechanisms).

4. *Cranes/large-scale equipment* This is normally a one-off assembly; small quantity batches or continuous production lines.

    Usually this will involve large-scale fabrication shops (metal cutting and welding), machine shops, purchasing of specialist items (electric motors, control equipment, etc.), that are then assembled and fitted together.

46

The distinction usually accorded assembly and fitting is that assembly is the easy putting together of different parts and sub-assemblies, using fixing arrangements which are quick to use—strict control over quality of parts is essential.

Fitting involves the modification of parts to enable them to be brought together satisfactorily. Fitting is used either when the quality of production is poor, necessitating modification to get the pieces to fit together (a very undesirable practice) or when it is important that two parts need mating together in such a way that they behave together in a precise, uniform way (this is still undesirable, but may be the most economical way of assembly).

It can be seen that the whole mode of assembly is dependent not so much upon how the layout and line have been put into operation, but upon the total manufacturing concept—What is the service the company is setting out to provide? This in turn depends not only upon the specialist knowledge and financial resources within the company, but also upon that part of the total market which the top management in the company has chosen to service. Management has discovered a market need or market sector to service.

SUB-ASSEMBLIES

The least costly way to put products together is to make final assemblies out of sub-assemblies, and not directly out of all the individual parts that are needed.

Final assembly should always be a very quick and efficient procedure. Keeping work away from final assembly should always be the aim, this keeps workers away from one another, it also means that any deficiencies in parts production are kept away from the final assembly. It is much better and easier to check individual parts or sub-assemblies *before* they are assembled, otherwise it may necessitate taking things to pieces again, a most undesirable and uneconomic practice. The fewer tests and checks that can be designed into the final product the better.

MAKING OR PURCHASING IN BATCHES OR CONTINUOUSLY

When items are made in batches, a large quantity is made together, and then placed into stock, from which a service to assembly/sub-assembly or to a customer is provided. When final assembly as continuous assembly is used, often it is better to relate sub-assembly and finishing processes to that continuous process, but time-phased with that final assembly.

47

For manufacturing of parts for the continuous production process it is necessary to consider:

1. Will the parts be made at a much faster rate than they are needed for assembly?

2. Is there a setting-up time needed? The longer the setting-up time, the greater the need for batching.

3. Are there key machines, which need 'close' scheduling in order to maintain supply and economical use of any high investment?

4. Are the materials available continuously or are they brought in batches.

Here it is important to stress that the manufacturing plan for assemblies should be based primarily on what is needed, rather than what the production department wants to make. This is the whole concept of materials requirements planning (MRP), Kanban and period batch control (PBC)—compared to EBQ manufacture or EBQ/EOQ used in the stock control concept of manufacturing planning.

It takes a higher value to justify making parts continuously than to assemble parts continuously.

Other considerations in parts manufacture are:

1. What kind of service is needed for the parts manufacturing operation?

2. What kind of investment/specialization can be justified for the volumes involved?

3. Should there be overlapped or gapped operations?

4. What kind of control is necessary?

5. Can parts be grouped together for more economical manufacture?

With much of modern production, the key parameters seem to be:

1. The demand of products arising from the policy set by top management for the market sector serviced.

2. The economic justification for investing in more specialized plant and equipment to meet that demand.

With many of the recent technical advances in robotics, flexible manufacturing systems, computer aided manufacture such as numerical control of machine tools, more flexibility is introduced, and the requirement for large size batch production reduced considerably. The aim should be for a more flexible total manufacturing system geared to the 'total' policy concept for the company.

Production control

The second of the principal problem areas of manufacturing management, namely production control, is covered in this chapter. Production control encompasses a wide range of activities and responsibilities, from providing assurance on resource availability to meet market demands to monitoring and controlling the flow of the product as it progresses through its several stages of manufacture in order to meet known delivery schedules and cost restraints. The first four sections deal with different aspects. The basic principles involved in operating an effective production control system are discussed in Sec. 3.1. The way in which it should be organized in a company often gives rise to different viewpoints and this is the subject of Sec. 3.2. Its essential functions and responsibilities are raised in Sec. 3.3; while the documentation and paperwork aspects are discussed in Sec. 3.4. Section 3.5 looks at the capacity needs generated by a production plan, and Sec. 3.6 at input controlled shop scheduling. Lastly Sec. 3.7 is concerned with controlling output.

The effectiveness of any production control system depends largely on the nature of the systems developed, the way in which it is organized and the scope of its authority in a given organization. It is essential that attention should be paid to these issues in order to achieve the desired company performance. Also included in Sec. 3.4 is the question of organizing maintenance operations as in many situations this, along with production control, forms an integral part of the overall manufacturing control system.

3.1 Principles of effective production control

The aim is to survey the whole field of production control, as practised in the United Kingdom in particular, but to include recent developments from the United States and Europe. Readers can assess for themselves the implications for their own companies and hopefully make worthwhile changes for effective control of manufacturing.

There is little doubt that when simple, but good, production control systems are installed in companies, the overall productivity of a factory is usually increased by 30 per cent or more. However, it is not systems alone that will secure these results. It is of even greater importance to make sure that well-trained and professional production controllers are running the systems effectively. Production control can be applied to many different industries—electrical, manufacturing, food, clothing, printing, cosmetics, pharmaceutical, furniture, and so on. But no two companies are alike, even if they are from the same industry, or the same group of companies making identical products.

It is therefore imperative that production control systems are designed and tailormade for the particular company and that these are practical in every respect.

One of the main reasons why computer systems of production control are often ineffective is because in the first place they have been poorly designed by computer specialists—people who know a lot about computers, but who are not production control specialists.

Production control specialists are people who know where to look for causes of problems, to set realistic objectives for attainment, and who are skilled at planning and providing for those plans.

The main problem areas that they are able to resolve are:

1. Delivery promises which are infrequently met.
2. Build-up of work in progress in key areas of the factory.
3. Too many mixtures of small and large batches which cause havoc on the shop floor.
4. Vast resources of cash locked away in finished stocks, part stocks or materials.
5. Long throughput times, where requirements and plans are not co-ordinated effectively.

These are the practical problems that are often met in industry and which usually require practical solutions.

How are companies dealing with these problems today? What systems have companies been putting into operation of late and how effective are they in these areas? These are questions which we will have to discuss.

WHAT IS PRODUCTION CONTROL?

Production control has been defined in British Standard 3138:1959 as:

Procedures and means by which manufacturing programmes and plans are determined, information issued for the execution and data collected and recorded to control manufacture in accordance with the plans.

Material control can also be defined as:

Procedures and means by which the correct quantity and quality of materials and components are made available to meet production plans.

A production controller has been defined as a person who ensures that the right products, of the right quality, at the right cost are produced and delivered at the right time. The main problem is to define precisely what the word 'right' refers to, and its relevance in a particular organization.

The emergence of the materials management concept as an integrated management approach is a development which arose from the widespread recognition of the problems created when the control of materials is separated under divided or dispersed functions and responsibilities.

EFFECTIVE PRODUCTION CONTROL

The flow of work in balanced batches to predetermined plans to meet due dates is effective production control.

If the flow stops we generally get queues, shortages or surplus elsewhere, uneconomic utilization of assets and cash tied up in stocks and work in progress.

3.2 Organization of production control

The purpose of a production control department in a manufacturing unit is to combine a number of different activities into a related and coherent role, such that the control of manufacturing and the supply of materials and parts are co-ordinated and thoroughly prepared in advance.

The planning and control of manufacturing are often very complex. From the viewpoint of sales, success depends to a large extent on providing a balance between market demand for standardized products and specific orders for variations on a basic product; from the viewpoint of production, utilization of plant, labour and other manufacturing resources is important; effective utilizing of cash resources through economical stock levels and material flow is essential financially.

Imbalance occurs because: (a) product demand fluctuates; (b) customers want absurd modifications to the product; (c) machines breakdown; (d) labour is unavailable through stoppages, lost time or recruitment problems; (e) cash resources are tight and cost a lot of money; and (f) materials are

51

difficult to procure on time. The job of the production controller is to minimize the effect of all these problems, and indeed to overcome them where practical, so that deliveries are on time and the company achieves the return on assets desired as an investment. The number of variables present in a manufacturing unit is usually considerable. These can be:

Different products and variations
Different processes and operations
Parts and materials
Different quantities desired by customers

These have to be optimized within the limitations of:

Plant and equipment
Quantity and skills of people
Availability of money

So usually there is a complex situation in reaching a practical production plan. There is also an important consideration that the production programmes usually have to be planned quickly, otherwise the manufacturing would overtake the planning process.

Once the plan is in operation, progress must be monitored and correction applied to cope with changes as they occur. Unfortunately, some of these changes are self-induced by inefficient management practices, and others are completely unavoidable internally.

The assumption made in maintaining a production control department is that the investment of cash in salaries, paperwork and systems produces a worthwhile return in terms of greater throughput, better utilization of assets, and therefore higher profits than would be the case without such a department.

What are the corollaries of the above?

1. If production control is to be effective, it has to be important in an organization, and must receive support from all levels of management. It should therefore be the responsibility of a senior manager. Many of the best companies for production control have someone at board level, or at a level which has direct access to the boardroom. In other cases, it is the responsibility of the general factory manager (who has overall control of a unit). If top management would regard it as important, and ensure that it is done properly, then there is a better chance it will succeed.

2. If production control is to be effective, it has to be manned by effective people who are trained, experienced, competent and professional.

3. If production is complex, so too will be the production control system and levels of staffing required. Production control procedures are often simplified considerably and staffing levels reduced through reorganizing what the manufacturing unit is doing.

Examples of this are:

1. Rationalization of products.
2. Group technology or cell layout.
3. Specialization and standardization of activities.
4. Scientific stocking policies.
5. Simplified manufacturing processes (i.e., low-cost automation).
6. Smaller manufacturing units (where large, complex units exist).

DEFINING OBJECTIVES

All good systems design should start by defining the objectives—What is to be achieved?—although some statements of objectives are not often thought out sufficiently and they are not pertinent and specific enough. It is generally regarded that it is this area of activity which needs closely defining before real progress can be made.

Some statements are more obvious in theory, but much more difficult to accomplish in practice, e.g., on time deliveries to customers. It is often pertinent to keep a record of objectives' criteria by which deliveries are measured and set attainable targets for achievement.

For instance:

95 per cent of deliveries on time
3 per cent within one week of time
2 per cent within two weeks of time

Further definitions are then required—What is delivery? Is it when a manufacturing order is complete? Is it the date of dispatch? Or is it the date of arrival at the customer?

With regard to finished goods inventory, it is often pertinent to measure scientifically the service levels required against the values held in inventory. These can be calculated and a policy decision then has to be made regarding the service level required.

Objectives for throughput times in various sections, cost centres or departments will need defining. They should relate to the value of the work in progress, and perhaps to the system of ordering on to production, i.e., by economic batch sizes or by material requirement planning or by standard batch control techniques.

53

The objectives for production control must also be established for budgets of manufacturing against particular programmes as well. Standard costs for manufacturing can easily be exceeded by having too many alternative methods, additional overtime, too much scrap, too many split batches, too small or too large batch quantities.

One often hears the cry that in production control one cannot win. In management one has to win, i.e., achievement of delivery dates or bringing supplies in on target. However, because of the impact of so many variables, one cannot win all the time, and therefore suitable probabilities of achievement have to be set.

WHAT IS PLANNING?

Planning is essentially a process of preparing for the commitment of resources in the most economical fashion, and by preparing or allowing this commitment to be made faster and less disruptively.

The decision making which follows the development of plans involves allocation of money, men, materials and machines and commits the company in the real world.

Planning is a thought process, involving ideas, words and paper models. Our thought processes can be wrong—acceptance of facts and the truth. Is our planning 'pie in the sky' or realistic?

WHAT IS CONTROL?

From various views expressed in textbooks, there seems to be a common definition of 'control' which is in essence the following stages:

1. Determine a standard (performance, plan, target, objective, budget).
2. Obtain actual result (achievement).
3. Compare standard with actual.
4. Obtain difference.
5. If significant, report to person responsible.
6. Take corrective action.

Between 1 and 2 there should be communication, which in many organizations is much neglected. It need hardly be stated that if the football team doesn't know where the goal posts are, they cannot be blamed for not scoring the goals.

However, control in practice is much more than this. It can be compared with driving a car between points A and B, but it is important for the driver to keep his eyes on the road in order to anticipate any hazards or stoppages which might occur, and take corrective action before obtaining the actual result.

Much in modern management practice is sitting at a desk waiting for results and reports, from which corrective action and blame can be apportioned, this is similar to making a car journey with a driver who only looks in the rear-view mirror.

PRODUCTION CONTROL MODULES

Production control techniques are like Meccano pieces in a set; each defined piece can be fitted together in 'modules' to fit the needs of each individual company. Every company is different and needs different modules of production control to plan and solve its problems.

However, great care has to be taken in selecting the modules or principles that are relevant to a particular situation, which often package, modular and universally adaptable production control systems fail to achieve. They are implemented with sincerity and great effort, but unless there are professional people who know what they are doing, there is no real improvement in attainment of results.

However, it is generally recognized that production control can be broken down into respective modules of activity, which are to be discussed more fully under the following titles:

1. Demand forecasting.
2. Aggregate planning.
3. Production planning.
4. Manufacturing control and documentation.
5. Production scheduling.
6. Expediting.
7. Production reporting.

3.3 The function of production control

The purpose of having a production control department in a company is to bring together a number of necessary activities into one logical organization. These activities are concerned with the interpretation or identification of a manufacturing requirement and the translation of that requirement into a plan which utilizes the production department efficiently. There is no one method of doing this which is equally applicable to all companies—indeed each company will develop its own particular method—but there are a number of principles which should be considered whatever the size or complexity of a company. In small companies many functions may be carried out by a department—but either way, a clear understanding of these functions is necessary.

This section sets out to describe the activities which are logically associated in the production control department. It describes how that department is organized internally and how it fits into a wider manufacturing/company structure. It must be emphasized, however, that in any human enterprise, the strength and character of individuals will play an important part in the final organization. This is acceptable providing the logic of the situation is satisfactory and understood by all who are working together.

In conclusion, the professional responsibilities of the production control manager will be stated.

PRODUCTION CONTROL ACTIVITIES

Sources of information

In order to carry out its responsibilities within the company, the production department needs to know:

1. What to make.
2. How much/many to make.
3. When the product is required for sale.

The question as to 'what to make' and 'when it is required' will come from the marketing and sales department and again in 'language' that is meaningful to the production unit.

It is the responsibility of the production control department to receive this information from design and sales on behalf of the production unit. Should the information not be available—which it seldom is—or should the production department not be able to understand it—which it frequently cannot—then it is the responsibility of that department to ensure that the situation is rectified—only results are acceptable—no reasons or excuses as to why it cannot be obtained. In order to achieve this it is frequently necessary for the production control manager to invest a great deal of his time in close liaison with the relevant departments to ensure that they understand his requirements and are willing to co-operate with him in achieving the effective transfer of information. This will involve the acceptance of common procedure, time scales, units of measurement, coding systems, etc., and almost certainly, effective feedback of information from production to design and sales. The design is clearly necessary to enable production to know in detail what to make. Every component material must be defined and this invariably leads to much information having to be communicated. In order to achieve this, all suitable methods must be examined with a view to choosing the most effective one. As no design is perfect, the requirement and feedback information is essential. The 'quantity' of information from sales is equally important, but while the design is able to be accurately specified, the quantities may only be 'forecasts', or informed guesses. Here then production needs to know what the long-term plans are as well as the likely accuracy of the forecast figure, e.g., 1200 per month ± 5 per cent or 1200 per month ± 80 per cent, and a close liaison between sales and production control is vital if the nature of the forecast is to be understood.

The development of the production plan

The first step towards a production plan is to develop for each product—as defined by design—a 'production philosophy'. For example, will the product be made for stock in anticipation of orders, or will it be made continuously? Clearly the product itself or the industry may determine this but there are many occasions where there is an option and that option needs to be resolved. During this process, the 'materials philosophy' will also begin to develop. Do we propose to stock raw materials or shall we buy them for each and every order? Again the product and industry may determine this, but in any event, we are able to formulate an idea of how long it will take to make each product.

Based on the required date for the availability of the product, we can then begin to establish when we should start work to meet that date. In practice each product will require labour, plant capacity and material, and these may have to be shared by some or all of the products. It is therefore necessary to determine how each of these products will be loaded on to the available capacity to achieve the desired result.

Thus the production plan provides the input to the load, but because the capacity is limited the product plan itself may have to be revised. This planning, loading and replanning process may have to be carried out many times to arrive at a satisfactory overall plan. In practice, techniques exist which help to simplify the process of producing a production plan.

Plant capacity

In order to create a detailed production plan, it is necessary to know the capacity of the plant being loaded. This is sometimes easy as with, say, a fully automatic bottling plant with a designed production rate of 120 bottles a minute—but equally it is sometimes difficult as with, say, a manually operated centre lathe turning components to close limits. Here the plant capacity is a function of the competence of the operator, his incentive to get the job finished, and the ability of the machine to perform to the required limits. Detailed knowledge is required but even then it is frequently necessary to find a simple way—or a broad measure—on which to base the plan.

Capacity is almost always a function of time and hence we must also determine our policy with regard to shifts—Shall we work one, two or three? With regard to overtime—shall we work on Sundays? We must determine policy also with regard to new investment or the sub-contracting of excess loads. These are the ways in which we can alter the capacity.

Labour availability

There was a time when the capacity of the labour force was easily adjusted to suit the needs of a company. This situation still exists in some industries, the building trade for example, and in some countries; but more and more, job security is becoming socially necessary and hence 'labour capacity' more difficult to adjust.

We must therefore reconsider our old philosophies towards machine utilization and concentrate more on the constant loading of the labour force assuming that this can be made sufficiently adaptable to meet the changing load situation. Again, in practice, many techniques are available to help us determine the 'capacity' of the labour force, not the least of which is previous experience.

Material management

Essential to the smooth running of any production plan is the availability of materials. So closely is this allied that the control of the materials flow must be the responsibility of production control. The evaluation of the materials requirement from the production plan, the control of stocks, the determination of the net requirement, the arrangements for purchasing, goods inwards and stores are all essential activities of that department. Furthermore, these activities require information creation and handling of extraordinary accuracy. It is not unusual to have millions of pieces of information in a materials control system. An error rate of 1 in 1000 would lead to thousands of errors in just such a system and this is not acceptable.

It is therefore essential to the production control department that disruption to the production plan through shortages is avoided.

The control of manufacture

Production control is not responsible for making the product. This is the responsibility of the production manager. Production control is, however, responsible not only for creating the production plan and organizing an environment in which it can succeed, but also for reporting on the progress of production against the plan. This calls for feedback with the plan, and a report made on the corrective action to be taken as a result of deviations from that plan.

The organization of the production control department

The activities outlined above can be brought together in many ways but the organization shown below is typical in a medium to large production unit. For a smaller unit one man may be doing the job of several men.

Production control manager

- Production controller
- Materials requirement
- Planning section
- Scheduling section
- Materials control section

The place of production control in the organization

The production control manager, responsible as shown above, should report to the senior production executive along with the production manager, industrial engineering manager, etc. He does, however, need to have a very wide understanding of company operation to enable him to communicate with all departments of the business—sales, design, accounts, personnel, etc.

3.4   Production control systems and documentation

The purpose of this section is to review the type of production control paperwork systems which may be used in a typical factory. One point to consider is that no two factories have the same product parts, materials, processes or operations, and therefore the paperwork system will need to be different and suited to individual needs. There are generally three different categories of paperwork in a production control system:

1. Those which are needed prior to and in preparation for actual manufacturing; these are the production planning and scheduling functions.
2. Those performed in direct support of and during manufacturing; these are the production control functions.
3. Those concerned with control of the physical materials; these are the materials handling and storage functions.

The design and style of paperwork in a PC system will depend on the means of reproduction of basic forms. Generally there is an evolutionary chain as companies extend the use of technology to support their administration. These stages would be typically:

1. Hand written, manual systems.
2. Using a spirit duplicator to reproduce copies.
3. Using a photocopier and masking procedure to reproduce copies.
4. Using a word processor to produce copies.
5. Using a computer to produce copies or to view information directly from the screen.

Linked to the type of reproduction equipment would be the method of holding the master data for production control documentation.

Typical of master data is the following:

Product codes
Product description
Part or materials codes
Part description and specifications
Unit of issue
Quantity of issue per cost code
Operation number
Operation description
Cost centre
Operation time
Setting of make-ready time
Tooling required

Two main documents are produced from this type of data:

1. *Materials list* (including parts listing).
2. *Operations list.*

From the orders that are received from customers, and depending on the type of production system (mass production, batch production, one-off production and make to stock, make to order groupings, make to customer's order) the *master production plan* has to be formulated. This is usually a compromise between the demands of sales, the capacity of production, and the availability of finance. From this master production plan, *production plans* are needed for each department in the factory. These are usually linked to *works order documentation*. This is usually a card on which details of the order, the quantity to be made, the time when it is required, and the order numbers are specified. This is often linked to a listing of the operation list (from the master data).

Linked to the master production plan, is a *materials requirement plan*, and parallel to the works order documents is issued a *materials requisition* to withdraw materials or parts from the stores. When parts are being made, there is often one material item for every requisition; when assemblies or sub-assemblies are being made, there is usually a number of items per requisition. In this case, 'kitting' the parts and materials together for common issue from the stores is made.

Work in progress documents are then needed to record the progress of work through the factory. On each document will be the starting and issuing quantity, the stage-by-stage booking of quantities and scrapped quantities as the work progresses, and the finishing quantity as the completed work is booked into the stores.

This produces a production control record of what has been produced, and when, and is used as a comparison with the production plan to find exceptions and monitor results. In smaller companies the record can be provided on the reverse of the works order documentation.

For the basic material flow, the following documents will be needed:

1. Goods received note.
2. Receipt into stock note.
3. Stock card.
4. Requisition (for authorization of issue).

With the use of computerized systems these basic records will be amended to suit the requirements of the factory; but the basic means of planning and control will have to remain, although in a slightly different way.

It is important to remember to keep all documentation as simple and straightforward as possible. The basic systems described above are not too difficult to maintain; however, when the basic system is expanded to include different documents for each operation, each transfer stated, etc., then often there is too much paperwork in the system for people to control adequately; and as a result the whole system gets into disrepute.

The whole basis must therefore be the one based on the KISS profile (keep it simple stupid).

Needless to add that a professional look at the paperwork procedures by an organization and methods analyst, who is competent at manual systems design, systems equipment, forms design and operation manuals will normally produce a far more competent result than the often seen process of adding extra pieces of paper here and there, as needs seem to arise.

3.5 Capacity requirement planning (CRP)

Total capacity planning has these main levels:

1. *Resource planning* Stemming from aggregate production planning based on business plans for products and markets. Do we have enough production capacity in the future?

2. *Rough cut capacity planning* This interacts with the production schedule master (MPS) to predict which facilities represent potential capacity problems.

3. *Capacity requirements planning (CRP)* Looks at the MRP requirements and generates load requirement on work centres.

LEAD TIMES

Capacity management and lead times in a manufacturing company must be carefully managed. The different types of lead time are the following:

Manufacturing lead time

This comprises two components:

1. *Order release lead time* This is the time needed to reach the first operation from the date a works order is raised for production.

2. *Order lead time* This is the time from the beginning point of the first operation to the point where the batch is received into the stores.

Purchasing lead time

This comprises:

1. *Order release lead time* Prior to placing an order.

2. *The delivery lead time* From the placing of an order until the goods are received.

3. *Preparation lead time* This is the time elapsed between the receipt of goods, through incoming inspection, checking quantities/weights, placing into storage containers and placing into stock. If there is material requisition, or if kitting time is needed, these times must be allowed for in the lead time calculations.

The lead times normally quoted by suppliers comprise delivery lead times only.

In capacity requirements planning, we are concerned primarily with manufacturing lead times. In order to control lead times it is necessary to manage capacity through careful planning, order release and order control.

Order lead times include the following:

1. Queuing time on a work centre prior to the operation. This will be dependent upon the releasing of work to the work centre which must be managed well.

2. Setting time for the batch.

3. Operation/processing time.

4. Transport time (including any checks, waiting following on operation and the taking of goods from one works centre to another).

In order to computerize CRP the following files of information are necessary:

1. *Routing file* This comprises information about making the part or assembly such as: operation number, cost centre and work centre, setting time per batch, operation time per piece.

2. *Work centre file* This is composed of information about each work centre: work centre reference number, description, capacity in hours, utilization index, number of machines or people, etc.

The output information from CRP is in the form of expected loads on each work centre, usually week by week. CRP is *not* shop scheduling.

CALENDAR FILE

This is where days or weeks are expressed in a matrix or grid (with holidays and non-working periods marked so that they are not loaded).

It is also usual not to load the complete capacity during such an exercise.

1. To allow some flexibility for future changes and insertions, but of a defined level. Constant insertions and deletions *ad lib* cause terrible problems for production controllers and customers in the long run because of the unreliability this normally creates.

2. To allow for known down-time, e.g., repairs, shortages, etc., which occur in every factory. It is often necessary to measure the utilization of equipment to find the 'index' to be used, e.g., 0–80 utilization index or load 35 hours for a 40-hour-week.

Capacity can also be measured in terms of machinery or manpower, whichever is the key factor to be considered.

Machine shops—normally by machines
Press shops—normally by machines
Processing plant—normally by equipment
Assembly—normally by manpower

63

The balancing of demand to capacity is a 'key' factor in effective performance. Control of business levels and of factory effectiveness is possible through capacity management; it is not the detailed planning and scheduling through the shop or department.

It is likened to a town split by a river with a single bridge. At certain times of the day—morning for going to work and school, and evenings when finishing for the day—if all are 'let loose' on the bridge together, then confusion and traffic jams result.

If the traffic to the bridge could be regulated either by staggered starting and leaving times or by controlling the traffic flow prior to its reaching the bridge then the traffic flow over the bridge would be more organized and would keep moving. A similar situation applies in industry. (A further possibility is to build another bridge.)

Too much work on the shop floor creates the following:

Confusion
Delays
Unpredictability
Money tied up

3.6 Input control and shop scheduling

INPUT CONTROL

The control of orders input to manufacture is a function of available inventory and work in progress already on the shop floor. It can be subdivided into the following:

1. *Order release* This is the selection and issuing of the production orders into the production department. It is based on the production plans, the availability of materials and parts, and the expected rates of production. It is important that they are issued at the rates that the production department can handle them otherwise large overloads will result.

2. *Scheduling orders* Assigning starting and finishing dates to the operations to be performed (see below).

3. *Loading the orders* Developing the total hours required in each time period for all operations scheduled in each work centre. If computerized CRP is in use, this job will have already been accomplished.

64

SHOP SCHEDULING

This has been defined as planning the sequence in which specific operations for each works order should be carried out at work centres, for goals for starting and finishing times.

Some objectives could be:

1. Completion of orders by due date.
2. Minimum throughput time for all orders.
3. Maximum machine load each week.
4. Minimum machine idle time.
5. Minimum operator idle time.
6. Minimum costs.

Weightings are often used for some of these different factors in computerized systems, with manual override where necessary.

The types of data required for scheduling:

1. *Fixed data*   For example, SMs/100 off, machine speeds, capacity specifications.
2. *Historical data*   Stocks available, work completed by stages.
3. *Incidental*   Human and machine differences, breakdowns, absenteeism, quality.

All the latter are things which will affect every manufacturing unit; the day-to-day occurrences which disrupt the most perfect planning system. Plans are vitally necessary but they can go astray sometimes. Exception action is therefore necessary to put things right. The level at which this action is effective is not in the planning office away from the shop floor, but on or next to the shop floor itself.

The area of short-term scheduling of operations sequencing is normally one of the most complex in production control, and for this reason, many computerized production control (CPC) systems do not offer a module in this area, or if they do, it does not usually deal with the job very effectively.

IBM has for many years provided software for the more complex shop operations. It started with a German who wrote specialist software for this type of problem and was called 'KRAUS'. This was then modified and improved and the system called 'CLASS' was introduced (*capacity loading and scheduling system*), which was later changed with improved facilities to CAPOSS-E.

Another system which operates successfully in the scheduling areas is called MICROSS. This system is based on loading each work centre according to specially designed decision rules.

Each operation for each order is located on to the system, with interlinks for the relationships between operations, and between operations and assembly by way of a network structure. Each operation has allocated:

1. *A setting time*   For preparing work or the machine for use.

2. *Operation time*   Quantity × op. time per piece.

3. *Waiting time*   For inspection and administration, or obtaining transport.

4. *Transportation time*   Time to collect and carry to the next operation.

The computer then calculates for each load centre, the total load in hours and the load for each week number. Typically the first few weeks are overloaded, and as the weeks further ahead are considered, so the load gets progressively smaller. This is often expressed in tabular and in 'histogram' form and is planning with unlimited capacity.

Where necessary the computer will also calculate the 'queuing time' for each operation, when, for example, more than one job is waiting to be started on a particular machine.

FORWARD AND BACKWARD SCHEDULING

This is the part of scheduling which requires the more powerful type of computer. Capacity is fixed—no overloads are allowed, so the system has two options:

1. *Fixed capacity due date fixed*   Therefore the computer works from the final date backwards to find the optimum starting dates. This on the first run is often a few weeks previous to the present date.

2. *Fixed capacity start date fixed*   Here the computer works from the start of the operations and ends up with a final date for completion. This often ends up a few weeks after the required date.

Various options have then to be tried, such as overtime, off-loading and consideration of priorities. The better that capacity management is organized, the more fruitful scheduling is likely to become.

Output can be as follows:

− Work listed for each machine
− Material availability
− Tool availability
− Load statements
− Orders-on-hand statement
− Statistics for off-loading

SHOP FLOOR DATA COLLECTION

Sometimes called 'data pathing'. The main object of this is collection of up-to-the-minute details of output, work-in-progress and lost time for purposes of control.

Information from the shop floor often has more than one need:

1. Recording of production records, to check progress against plans.

2. Valuation and control of work in progress.

3. Summarized information for production management.

4. Recording of detail for incentive and wage payments.

5. Recording of details for standard costing, labour controls and variance reporting.

Computerized systems normally comprise robust, but easily operated, industrial terminals which are linked to a suitable controller (which can be an independent mini- or microprocessor-based system controller, or a variety of front-end/host processor combinations) which is linked directly to the main computer and its desk files.

The terminal, which is usually of rugged construction with a cast metal case and suitable masking or sealing to prevent deterioration by oil, dust, water or similar potential intruders, has facilities for:

1. Reading bar-coded operation cards.

2. ID badge cards.

3. Simple keyboard for entry of variable data.

4. Provision for suitable message types:

   (a) attendance;

   (b) work in progress;

   (c) waiting time;

   (d) goods in;

   (e) inspection;

   (f) rework;

   (g) stores issue;

   (h) exception, etc.

5. Display for characters entered.

6. Time check for automatic recording of date and time.

Other types of terminal are now being introduced for a variety of purposes, some of which are now 'interactive' with the system computer and its files.

67

Another recent advance is the use of microprocessor-based machine monitoring equipment. Sensors which are placed near to the running parts of a machine—such as a shaft—record when the machine is stopped or working. A simple keyboard is also used to indicate stoppage by reason of, e.g.:

Machine breakdown
Material not available
No work
Awaiting instructions
Inspection

A large number of machines can be linked from these sensors back to a host mini- or microcomputer which records and then display the results.

3.7   Controlling output

This function normally includes the following elements:

1. Ensuring that capacity is adequate to meet the plan, including short-term considerations.
2. Controlling queues of work and reducing lead times.
3. Balancing input and output rates in aggregate.
4. Providing early warning signals of the need for corrective action.
5. Reviewing priority consideration and rescheduling if necessary.
6. Flow control—the elements of which have been defined by Plossl as:
    (a) planned production levels of major activities;
    (b) well-defined 'in' and 'out' stations for materials;
    (c) clearly visible dating and identification of work in progress;
    (d) delay reports or slow money work;
    (e) priority system;
    (f) good housekeeping and shop floor discipline.

In many systems progress clerks and expediters are used to chase work which is in arrears. As a general rule, the more effective the planning, the less expediting there is, the more effective the system will be.

4

Materials control

This chapter concentrates on the third principal problem area of manufacturing management, namely, materials control. Most companies have vast sums of capital tied up in some form of stock or raw materials and a very significant percentage—sometimes as high as 50 per cent—of it in manufacturing costs comprising of direct materials cost. Therefore, based purely on the question of economics alone, materials management is a key area for control. In any typical organization several functions such as purchasing, stock control, warehousing and production control have a role to play in operating the materials management system. The way in which the various activities are co-ordinated between these specialist functions influences its eventual success in practice. Section 4.1 looks at the concept of developing an integrated materials management system and suggests one model form or organization. The managerial aspects of monitoring and controlling the amount of stocks held and ordered form the subject for Secs 4.2 and 4.3. Section 4.2 deals with the important aspects of inventory control techniques and the mathematical models available for making the most cost-effective decisions on how much and when to buy, and how much stock to hold. Section 4.3 deals with materials requirements planning as a tool which will provide a solid basis to deal with the planning and procurement of materials from one known demand for the final product. Section 4.4 is concerned with the methods of looking at aggregate inventories rather than individual items within that total inventory. Bearing in mind the important principle of having all the materials necessary for making some of the products rather than having some of the materials for making all the products, Sec. 4.5 deals with the crucial issue of expediting or 'progress chasing' of supplies and components. A vital area to control especially in achieving desired delivery dates for its own products, this section looks at the various courses of action that a company could take in this area.

4.1 Modern materials management

During the past decade there has been a change in the organizational structure of many companies, to make use of the function known as materials management. Many of the companies that have adopted this concept in the United Kingdom are of American parentage, but a few are British-owned concerns; Smiths Industries being one of these.

With the increased international market of most companies, and where many new methods of material handling and distribution have been fostered—such as containerization, container ships, new methods of bulk handling, new storage systems, the rapid development of air freight—these have all prompted the need for increased specialization in physical distribution management (PDM), separate from or within materials management (MM).

In many manufacturing companies the greatest resource commodities are materials, parts and other purchases. These can often amount to between 40 and 60 per cent of a company's total expenditure. It is important, therefore, that the management of expenditure is done professionally and well.

Within the United Kingdom, there has been a large increase in the number of new warehouses. All over the country one sees new development sites, and a large proportion of these are storage warehouses and distribution centres, a very much smaller proportion are new factories.

It looks as though we are rapidly becoming a post-industrial society, for better or worse. What is known is that materials management is a vitally important element in our new society.

WHAT CONSTITUTES MATERIALS MANAGEMENT?

Perhaps, first of all, we need a list of the functions which are often found under the materials management (MM) umbrella:

Inventory control
Invoicing
Order receipt and processing
Physical distribution
Production planning and control
Purchasing
Receiving
Shipping
Stores management
Transportation
Warehousing

Some of these functions overlap, for instance, physical distribution management can often be another umbrella for many of these, as can production control in a manufacturing concern.

The main point about the list is that each of these functions deals with materials. How any one company will organize itself for materials management will depend primarily on the type of company itself. A chain store group, a distribution company and a manufacturing concern will all have a little in common, but they will each be different, and considered to be different from the materials management viewpoint.

THE ADVANTAGES OF MATERIALS MANAGEMENT

If materials are the largest single resource in a company, then it is necessary that this resource should be managed well; and being the largest item of resource and expenditure, it needs expert attention and co-ordination.

When responsibility for materials comes under different functional heads in management, then they will not necessarily be treated with the same importance from the total company viewpoint because of sectional interests. For instance many purchasing officers may be prone to keeping large stocks of raw materials—this way they get less criticism from their colleagues for shortages in supply. The same goes for the manufacturing manager, who often wants to produce in large batches, so as to reduce machine setting time, and increase machine utilization. The sales manager is also prone to the same kind of forces, because if he can keep large stocks of finished goods then perhaps he can provide better customer service, and at least stop customer complaints about waiting for deliveries.

The above executives are, in all probability, waging war with the finance executives who want to reduce money tied up in the business. Which way is best for the company as a whole? And for the customer?

The first point to be made is that the largest stocks do not imply better customer service. In fact the reverse is often true. One frequently finds companies whose main stocks are of slow-moving items but who are fighting desperately for the items which most customers want.

We in the United Kingdom have tended to equate large stocks with customer service. In Japan the reverse is often advocated—good customer service is linked to fast response of materials flow with little stock. Such is the case with just-in-time techniques such as Nissan with their Kanban system. It must be emphasized that these systems do not always work, even in Japan!

What is important is that stocks are managed well—reducing the overall value of money, increasing the stock turnover and materials flow, and at the same time providing a better customer service. With the knowledge and skill of materials management techniques this can all be achieved, and is being achieved in many companies.

Take a typical case of stock turnover in a manufacturing company—stocks in this instance would include raw materials, work in progress, parts, stocks and finished goods stocks. If the cost of materials is 50 per cent of the net sales, then the following calculations can be made:

1. If sales turnover is £50 million (it could be £50 000 or just £5000, the argument is the same), and if stocks are turned over just twice a year, then the value of total stocks is £25 million. The value added on each £1 of sales is 50 pence—value added is then £25 million.

2. Therefore £25 million worth of stocks produces £25 million of value added.

3. If the stock turnover is three times per annum, then £16.7 million worth of stock produces £25 million of value added.

4. If the stock turnover is four times per annum, then £12.5 million worth of stocks produces £25 million of value added.

A smaller sum of money is being used over and over again to produce the same result—and often better results if the customer service is improved which leads to greater sales.

THE ORGANIZATION OF MATERIALS MANAGEMENT

The functions that are grouped together under the heading of materials management will differ in each company. What is most vital is that *all* major items of materials flow are co-ordinated together.

In a manufacturing concern, a typical arrangement for a larger concern would be like that of Fig. 4.1.

Quite frequently, however, an alternative arrangement is made as shown in Fig. 4.2—note only the MM functions are listed for the sake of clarity.

This kind of arrangement is often more suitable when, for example, there are many unit factories within manufacturing. In this case the unit factory manager would control the on-site production planning and control, the factory stores and stock control. Often co-ordinated with a central master production scheduling function where sales needs and factory capacities are balanced, and where a centralized materials management function still operates. Here, the materials management personnel set the guidelines within which the factory management operates. It is important to recognize that the factory manager is in overall executive control of his unit. He alone is responsible for this—within the goals, objectives and criteria set for the needs of the total company operation.

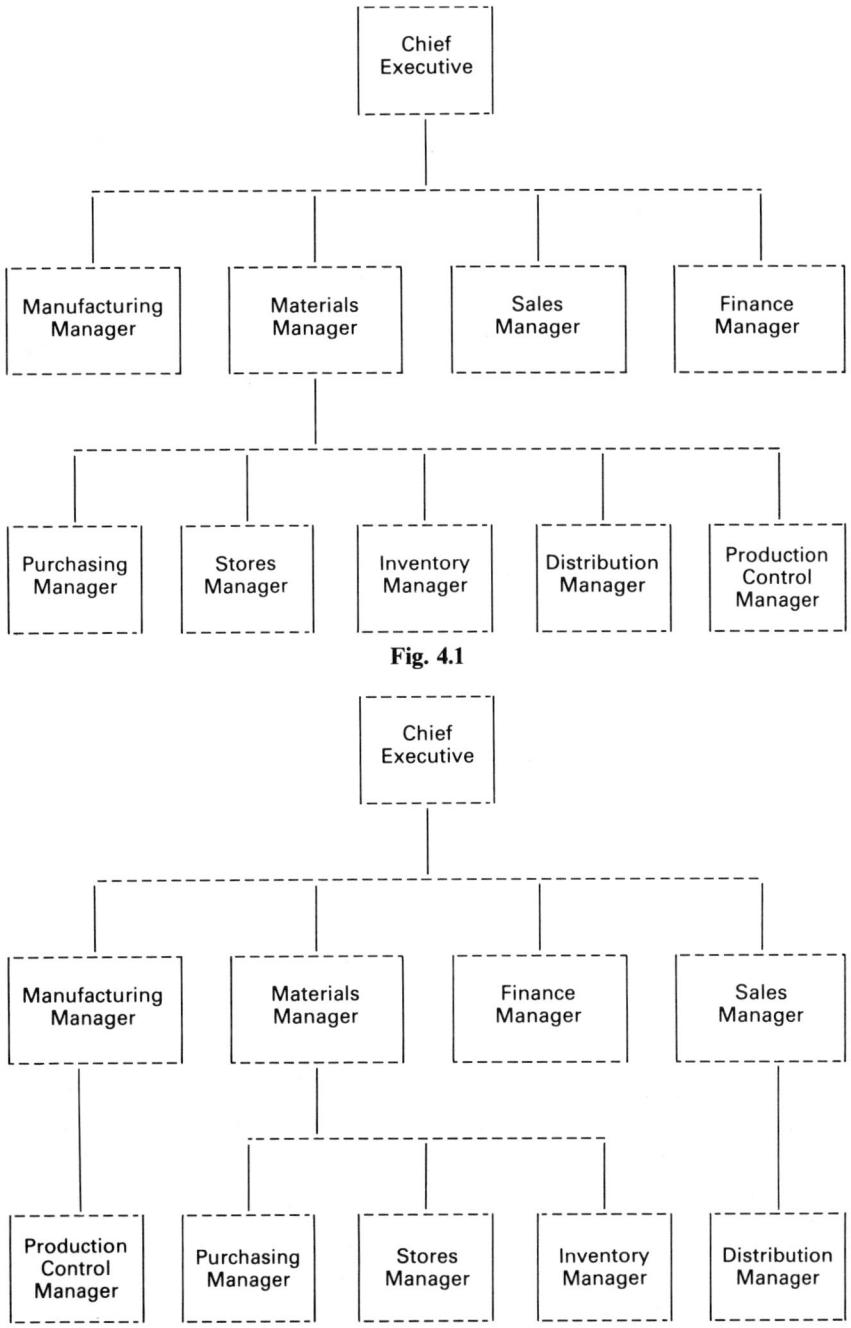

Fig. 4.1

Fig. 4.2

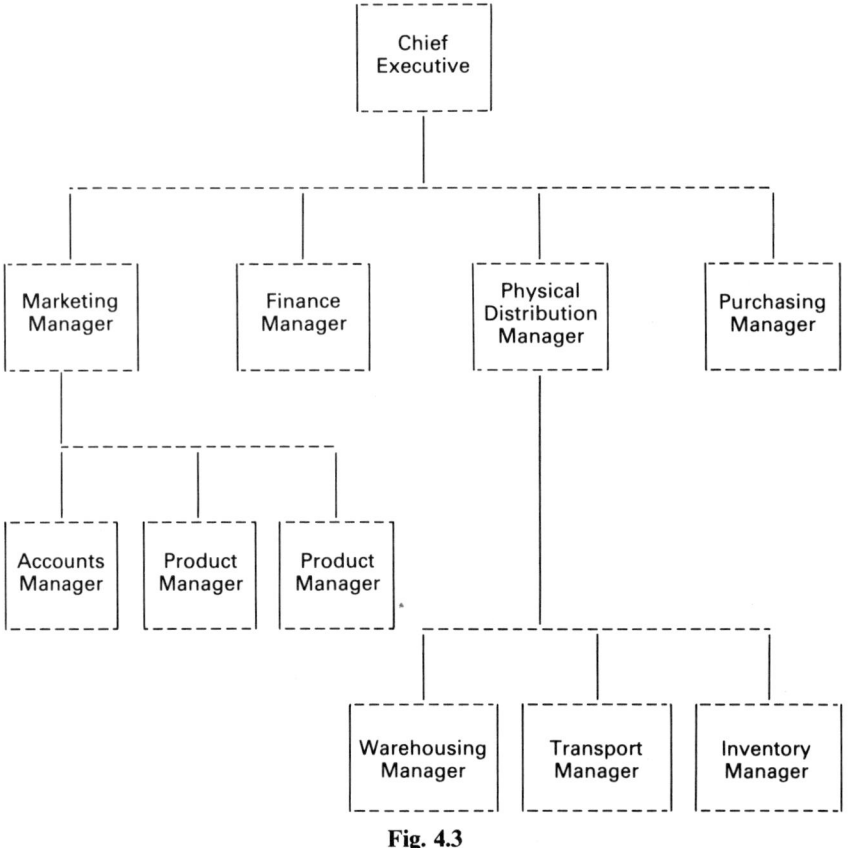

Fig. 4.3

In many distribution companies, there may be quite a different arrangement (Fig. 4.3).

In this case the physical distribution manager and the purchasing manager could be combined under an overall materials manager. But the overall concept here is slightly different. It is the product manager here who normally has the overall co-ordination for his own product range. He or she would manage the whole of the marketing, sales literature, direct selling and liaise with the materials manager for his own direct product requirements. It would be the product manager who decides what to market and sell, and therefore what to purchase and stock.

An accounts manager is also shown, because when companies are organized on a product management basis, they often have special managers for a few very large main customers. The co-ordinatory need for this becomes even greater. A top materials manager often provides a key role in this type of organization.

Functions within an organization need to change as companies need to change to external business opportunities. Functions should be organized so that they provide the most cost-effective and greatest market response for the total business operation. The organization of materials management should be considered on this same basis, viewed from the perspective of using professional materials managers and their skills in the best interests of the organization.

4.2 Inventory control

STOCKHOLDINGS

Stockholdings can be broken down into three categories:

1. *Working stocks* These are stocks which are held separately to meet a defined level of service. They are determined by reference to both the average demand (cycle stock) and the actual sales fluctuations about this average (safety stocks).

2. *Buffer stocks* These are the stocks held in addition to working stocks to accommodate differences between production capacity and maximum sales demand. They are used to maintain production levels during periods of low demand and to act as a reserve when sales demand outstrips production. They arise also during batch production when economic batch sizes are run to keep 'down-time', due to tool changing, etc., within reasonable limits.

3. *Policy stocks* These are the stocks which are acquired because they are available on the market at a very keen price, future supplies are uncertain or for other purchasing/financial reasons.

In this chapter we are concerned essentially with working stocks.

In considering any inventory problem, the first step should be to analyse the inventory range and to separate it into its individual segments. Both sales and inventories follow an 80:20 rule, where 80 per cent of sales are accounted for by 20 per cent of the items, the very fast movers (A) representing (say) the top 8 per cent of items; the medium movers (B) the next 12 per cent of items; and the slow movers (C) the remaining 80 per cent of items.

The graph (Fig. 4.4) shows a typical breakdown of sales.

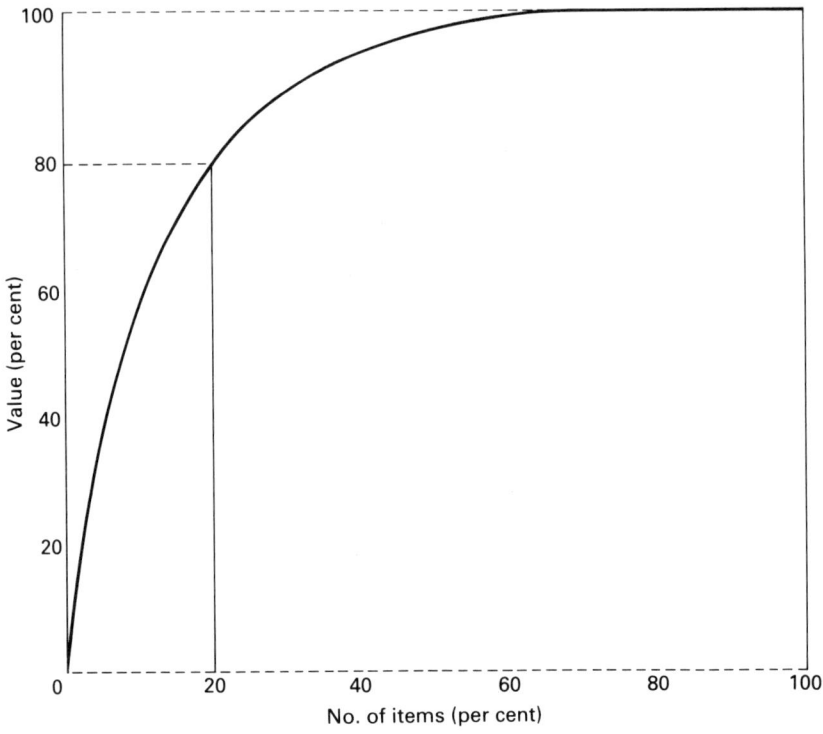

Fig. 4.4

WORKING STOCKS

These are made up of two components—the cycle stock and the safety stock. The cycle stock is determined by the average sales. For example, if the sales of one item were 100 per week at the rate of 20 per day, and a delivery from the supplier was made regularly first thing on a Monday morning, the stock would fluctuate between 100 and zero throughout the week and the average stock would be 50. In practice, however, the daily sales will fluctuate as will also the weekly sales, and an additional stock has to be kept to ensure that the item remains available. This additional stock is known as safety stock and its size will depend upon company policy towards the level of service, i.e., stock availability. It is also likely that, on occasions, the supplier will be late with his delivery and a further safety stock will need to be kept to meet this contingency.

When placing an order to replenish stock, the lead time of the supplier has to be taken into account. This lead time is the interval between raising the order and taking delivery of the goods.

76

TYPES OF RE-ORDER SYSTEM

There are two basic types of re-order systems:

1. *Re-order point*   A predetermined quantity is ordered when the inventory level falls below a certain value (the re-order point). The min–max system is a variant of this method in that the order quantity varies each time by the amount that the inventory falls below the minimum or re-order point.
2. *Re-order cycle*   Orders of varying quantity are placed (say) weekly to restore the in-hand and on-order inventory to a pre-determined level.

There is a difference between the two systems in the provision for safety stocks.

In re-order point systems, safety stock must provide protection during lead time period. In re-order cycle systems, this protection must be provided both during the lead time period and the review period. This system, therefore, gives rise to higher safety stocks.

Re-order point = average rate of usage during the maximum reasonable lead time plus safety stock

In re-order cycle systems, a maximum stock level has to be established to which quantity in-hand and on-order will be restored at each re-order cycle.

Maximum stock level = average rate of usage during a re-order cycle and maximum reasonable lead time plus safety stock.

Although re-order cycle systems lead to higher safety stocks, the disadvantages of re-order point systems must not be overlooked. These are:

1. Randomness of re-ordering.
2. Uneconomical orders (shipment of minimum order quantities).
3. Excessive ordering costs.

STANDARD DEVIATION

The calculation of safety stocks can be made only by recourse to statistical methods and probability theory. The abstract unit used to measure dispersion of values above the average is called the standard deviation represented by the Greek letter sigma (σ)

$$\sigma = \sqrt{\frac{\Sigma(x - \bar{x})^2}{n - 1}}$$

Where x = the value of any one result
$\bar{x}$ = the average result
n = the number of results
Σ = Greek symbol taken to represent 'the sum'

The standard deviation provides a means of establishing the probability that actual sales will exceed a specific sales level during a replenishment period. If actual sales over a number of periods are plotted in the form of a histogram, a bell-shaped curve can usually be drawn showing the dispersion about the average, known as the 'normal' curve. The standard deviation is a measure of the dispersion of the value about the mean, or in other words a measure of the 'flatness' of the curve (Fig. 4.5).

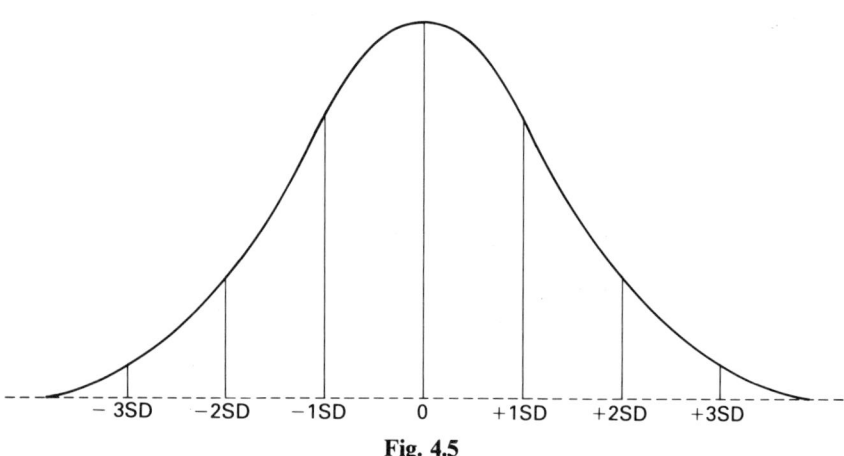

Fig. 4.5

It is a feature of all normal curves that the area enclosed by one standard deviation on either side of the average is 68.3 per cent, by two standard deviations 95.5 per cent and by three standard deviations 99.7 per cent.

By reference to statistical tables it is possible to determine the area enclosed by an intermediate value for the number of standard deviations, for example 1.75 or 2.30 which we will call K. This percentage area corresponding to any given value (in our case actual sales) will fall within plus or minus $K\sigma$ of the average level of sales. By providing a safety stock of $K\sigma$ (in addition to the cycle stock geared to the average sales level) we can avoid stock-outs for a corresponding percentage of time. We are, of course, concerned only with those sales that fall outside a range of $K\sigma$ above the average—there is no risk of stock-out for sales below the average.

Table 4.1 gives the level of service associated with different values of K.

78

Table 4.1   Levels of service associated with different values of K

K	Level of service (%)	K	Level of service (%)
0	50	1.56	94
0.52	70	1.65	95
0.84	80	1.75	96
1.04	85	1.88	97
1.28	90	2.05	98
1.34	91	2.33	99
1.41	92	2.57	99.5
1.48	93	2.88	99.8

It can be seen how rapidly the value of K rises as the level of service approaches 100 per cent. A level of service of 100 per cent is both theoretically impossible and economically impractical.

DETERMINATION OF SAFETY STOCKS

The determination of the standard deviation as expressed in the formula on page 77, is not easy to calculate without the help of computer facilities. Fortunately, an alternative measure of the dispersion, called the mean absolute deviation (MAD), can be determined using simple arithmetic and has a direct constant relationship to the standard deviation.

The mean absolute deviation (MAD) is the average of the absolute differences between individual values and the average of the values themselves.

$$\text{MAD} = \sum \frac{|x - \bar{x}|}{n}$$

Where $|\ |$ indicates that the arithmetical sign (i.e. $+$ or $-$) is disregarded and the remaining symbols have the meanings as in *standard deviation*.

Further

$$\text{MAD} = 0.8 \times \text{standard deviation}$$

In practice a good method of determining the standard deviation for each level of sales for a broad line of products with widely different rates of sale is as follows:

The MADs of a sample group within the product range are plotted against their average rates of sale on logarithmic paper. A straight line of best fit is then drawn through the scattered points. This is one on a sampling basis and an ABC analysis of unit sales by quantity (not value) will assist in obtaining a random sample across the entire range of unit sales.

The form of a typical average MAD line of best fit is shown in Fig. 4.6.

79

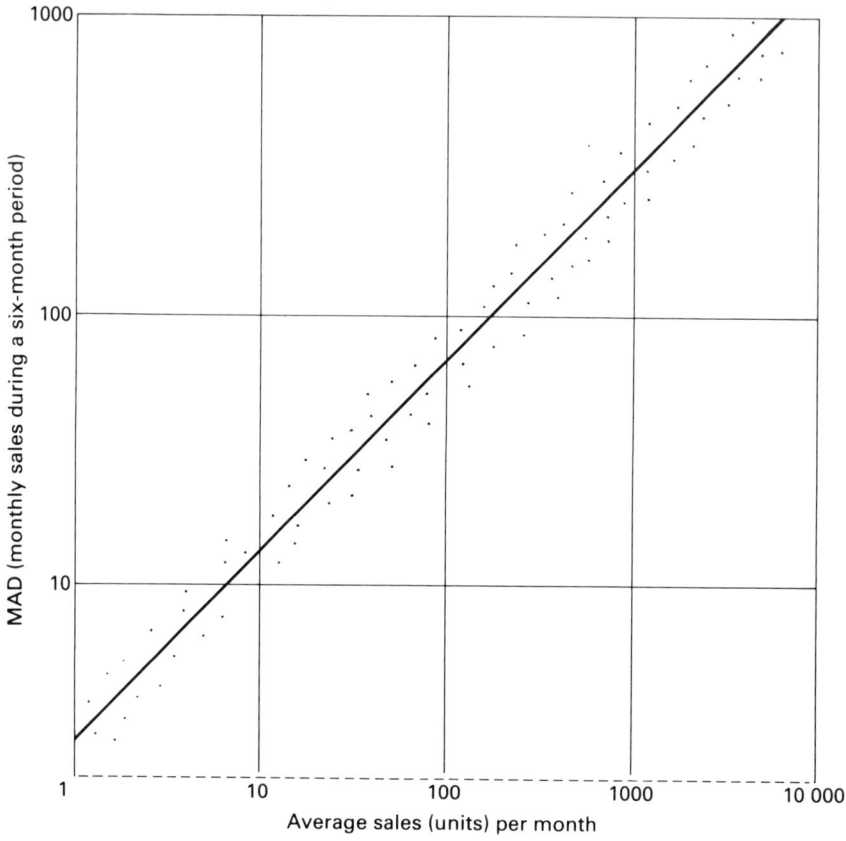

Fig. 4.6

The regression lines representing the average MAD at different levels of average sales show that items with high average limit sales have higher absolute variations in their sales but lower percentage variations.

The relationship between sales variations and average sales levels obtained by this plotting method normally results in fairly high correlation, when the sales variation and average sales are expressed in units. The same high correlation is not attained when money values are used.

Equal weeks of safety stocks for items with identical average annual money sales will usually provide different levels of protection where their volumes in units differ.

REPLENISHMENT SYSTEMS

There are several methods for replenishing branch inventories from a master warehouse. Two such methods are the imprest replenishment system and the allocation system.

1. *Imprest system* The branch warehouse stock is periodically replaced on a one for one basis. Stocks may be replaced (say) either weekly or fortnightly or when a suitable load has been accumulated. The problem lies in establishing the current normal inventory levels and revising these on a routine basis. The system eliminates the need for maintaining any record of branch inventories.

2. *Allocation system* The allocation system includes in each branch shipment a sufficient quantity of each item to rebalance the inventories— each item's inventory in hand and in transit will coincide with equal days of anticipated sales, all items will have the same run-out date. The problem here lies in updating average rates of sale, by, say, exponential smoothing methods and this calls for considerable calculation. The system allows for a much stricter control of inventory levels and any deliberate over-shipment in one period will be automatically compensated in later shipments.

Both systems have one drawback—they may call for the replenishment of impractical small quantities.

A combination of the two systems may be successful for a very broad product range. Fast running items (20 per cent of items, say) might be controlled by the allocation method and the slower moving items (80 per cent) by the imprest method.

ECONOMIC ORDER QUANTITY (EOQ)

Economic order quantity reconciles the cost of holding stock with the cost of ordering it. It indicates the correct quantity to order and is expressed by the formula:

$$Q = \sqrt{\frac{2as}{cv}}$$

Where a = cost of ordering
$\quad s$ = annual sales volume
$\quad c$ = carrying cost of stock
$\quad v$ = value/unit

The economic order quantity increases, therefore, as the square root of the total sales. As the quantity ordered has a direct bearing on the average

81

stock held it can be deduced that the stock required to service a given level of sales of a unit increases approximately as the square root of the volume of sales.

DESIGNING A RE-ORDER CYCLE SYSTEM

The following steps were recommended in a case history of a food wholesaler.

1. Fixed order day system   The placing of orders on the right day will minimize the supplier's lead times.

2. The stock of each line is considered weekly.

3. A maximum stock level point R is chosen for each line which is just high enough to avoid stock-outs during the lead time period plus a review period. The level R is chosen with reference to possible rates of sale and service levels. The actual stock in hand and on order is compared with the value R. A quantity equal to the difference is ordered, otherwise no action is taken.

4. Lead times (these varied from 2 days to 13 days: the longer the lead time the greater the variation). Control over lead time was exercised by the following equation:

$$\hat{L}_t = 0.1L_t + 0.9L_t - 1$$

Where $\hat{L}_t$ is the predicted average lead time at review period t
$\hat{L}_t - 1$ is previous predicted lead time
L_t is last observed lead time

5. Sales   A similar type of control was kept over the forecast of non-promotional sales.

$$\hat{S}_t = 0.1S_t + 0.9S_t - 1$$

Where $\hat{S}_t$ is the sales forecast
$\hat{S}_t - 1$ is the previous sales forecast
S_t is the last week's sale

6. Calculation of R.

$$R = (L + C)S + K\sigma_L$$

Where $\sigma_L^2 = (L + C)\sigma_s^2 + S\sigma_L^2$
and L is the predicted lead time in days
C is the review period in days $(= 5)$
S is the predicted sales per day
σ_s and σ_L are the standard deviations of sales and lead time
K is the factor relating to the level of service

σ_s and σ_L were derived using computer facilities and the equation was approximated to

$$R = (L + C)S + 4.4((L + C)S)^{0.5}$$

so that it could be manipulated manually.

SAFETY STOCK SAVINGS ARISING FROM A CENTRALIZED WAREHOUSE

As the demand for an item increases the safety stock, expressed as a percentage of annual sales, is reduced. Thus by centralizing storage, in particular of the slow moving items, considerable reductions can be achieved of total company stocks.

A centralized warehouse can also perform a valuable function where at branch level a few large orders are superimposed on a large number of small ones. The stock required to meet these large orders cannot be governed by the same system as that required to service the smaller orders, and to provide any reasonable level of service for the large orders, a vast amount of stock will need to be held at the branch. Bringing larger orders from the branches together in a central warehouse allows them to be serviced by a much smaller inventory.

In assessing the safety stock savings arising from centralization it is necessary to select a re-order interval. An interval of six weeks has been used in the calculations and this corresponds more or less with a stock turnover of 8. In essence the calculation goes through the following steps:

1. For an annual demand of D, divide by 8 to establish the expected demand in the re-order interval. Multiply the safety stock percentage at demand D by 8 to arrive at the branch safety stock.

2. Multiply the actual stock level found by (say) 15, representing the number of branches, to yield the total national safety stock.

3. Multiply the safety stock percentage at demand D by $\sqrt{\frac{8}{15}}$. This new percentage multiplied by the national demand, yields the centrally held safety stock.

4. Subtract this figure from the total branch safety stock, multiply the result by the average price at the demand D and divide by 10 to yield the savings (in pounds sterling) per annum for each item. This last calculation assumes 10 per cent to be the cost of capital.

4.3 Materials requirements planning (MRP)

A considerable amount of interest and attention to materials requirements planning is currently being given by companies on both sides of the Atlantic. By far the greatest amount of materials and parts used in manufacturing concerns are part of something else—the final product. The ingredients of foodstuffs, the parts used in an electronic assembly, the materials used in textiles, ceramics, pharmaceuticals and household chemical products are not needed at steady uniform rates throughout the year, but are related to the production plans of the final products. They have what is called dependent demand—the demand for the materials is dependent on the plans for the final product. Independent demand is where demand is unrelated to anything else the company stocks, this is usually the type of demand for final products.

Previously, many of the materials and parts that went into something else (the final product) were ordered on the basis of stock control records using re-order levels and re-order quantities. These levels were calculated from records of *past* usage and lead time. A dependent demand item can be calculated from the *future* plans of the end items. This is the philosophy behind materials requirements planning (MRP).

Materials requirements planning can apply to all types of products and processes involving multiple components. It is applicable: (a) to custom-built products like ships, aeroplanes and machine tools; (b) to manufactured and process production items such as cars, chemicals and packaged foodstuffs; and (c) to low or high volume batched products such as engineering and electronics. It therefore has wide industrial application.

The prerequisites for MRP are the following:

1. *A realistic master plan* This master plan drives the MRP. The master plan contains the end-item production quantities for each product and the time-scale for these. In computer terminology it is often called the master production schedule (MPS). All the derived plans from the MPS are invalid if the plan requires output beyond the capacity and facilities that exist.

2. *An accurate bill of materials (BOM)* The BOM contains the specification for all the parts and materials that comprise the final product. It is designed in such a way that the structure or relationships between the parts will be needed at different times to other groups of parts.

   The BOM forms the framework from which modern planning systems used in industry are derived.

   Accurate and up-to-date BOMs are necessary to produce realistic MRPs.

3. *Accurate stock information* Each stock item needs to be correctly identified with a unique number (stock or inventory code), and the current

accurate quantities held in stock (such as can be easily checked by a stock control) and the data necessary to describe the part accurately.

4. *Accurate information on orders already placed* An MRP will generate information for both made-in and bought-out components (or methods). Accurate knowledge of quantities already ordered and due dates is necessary if future orders are to be evaluated properly.

   The processing of data for successive operations or processes is *not* needed by MRP but this data is part of subsequent modules in most modern computer systems.

5. *Realistic lead times* The time required to procure or make an item is needed for reliability of MRP processing. Lead times can vary with batch sizes and with the workload on suppliers so careful scrutiny is needed.

6. *Careful batching considerations* Some processes are not batched, but most are and supplies from outside the company usually arrive in discrete groups (truck loads, boxes, sacks, containers, etc.). Batching of requirements needs to reflect the practical way in which the goods will be produced or delivered. Many MRP systems operate without going as far as batching, but in doing so leave out the very important control element on orders placed—internally or externally. The batched request can be the generated MRP requirements and this is valid if it is a realistic assumption.

There are other very important considerations in using MRP.

1. The computer programs and equipment need to handle vast volumes of data. The configuration (sizing) of the equipment must be adequate as must be the ability to input and access the data rapidly.

2. Accurate and timely reporting of information is essential. The procedure outside the computer system is important and needs careful design and implementation. People need proper training to appreciate what they are doing and to do their job properly. Materials issues and receipts, stock adjustments (should be avoided if possible) and order release and closing come under this category; as does the proper updating of information on the bill of materials files.

3. Discipline in identifying and controlling the batches of work once they are released on the shop floor.

4. Proper management planning and control over the plans, the systems ensuring timely execution (of those who fail!).

From the above details, it can be expected that many companies will experience problems in implementing such a system and this is the case. However, there are successes. In the United States, the University of Minnesota has completed a study of 326 companies, before and after computerizing production control. The results, which are averages, are shown in Table 4.2.

Table 4.2   Companies before and after computerizing production control

	Before	After
Lead time	64 days	57 days—cut 11%
Materials shortages	32%	21%
Delivery performance	64%	81%
Inventory turnover time per annum	× 3.5	× 4.7
Number of progress personnel	9.5	5.6
Reduction in overtime		14.5%

Perhaps a lot can or cannot be read into the figures in Table 4.2. However, what can be said is that there are signs of definite improvement in performance. The objective of MRP is to ensure that availabilities of component, sub-assembly and raw material inventories are able to support end-item production, with maximum cash utilization, so that balanced batches are ordered and controlled, taking into account stocks, orders in hand, batching rules and lead time.

There is other evidence from the United States which suggests that those who implement MRP successfully are the successful companies anyway— and that a good MRP system vastly improves the business results of those companies.

Table 4.3 shows that different sizes of company can implement MRP, but the larger companies are the most likely to have done so. As smaller systems are developed, so even smaller companies are using MRP today.

Figure 4.7 shows the flow of information into and out of a typical MRP system.

THE BILL OF MATERIALS

The bill of materials (BOM) gives the ingredients of a product, so does not contain the processing details as that information is kept on other files. The BOM is comprised of two main features:

The master information for each item
The structure

Table 4.3   Different-sized companies implementing MRP

Size criteria	Possible	Probable	Most likely
Sales	£5m	£5m–£15m	£15m +
Direct labour	200	200–600	600 +
Part numbers	2000	2000–5000	5000 +
Bill of material levels	1–2	3–4	5 +

Industry criteria

Food prod.	Textiles	Apparel
Tobacco	Rubber	Chemicals
Timber	Plastics	Metal prod.
Wood	Primary materials	Machinery
Paper	Pharmaceuticals	Electric
Clay		Transport equipment
Glass		
Stone		

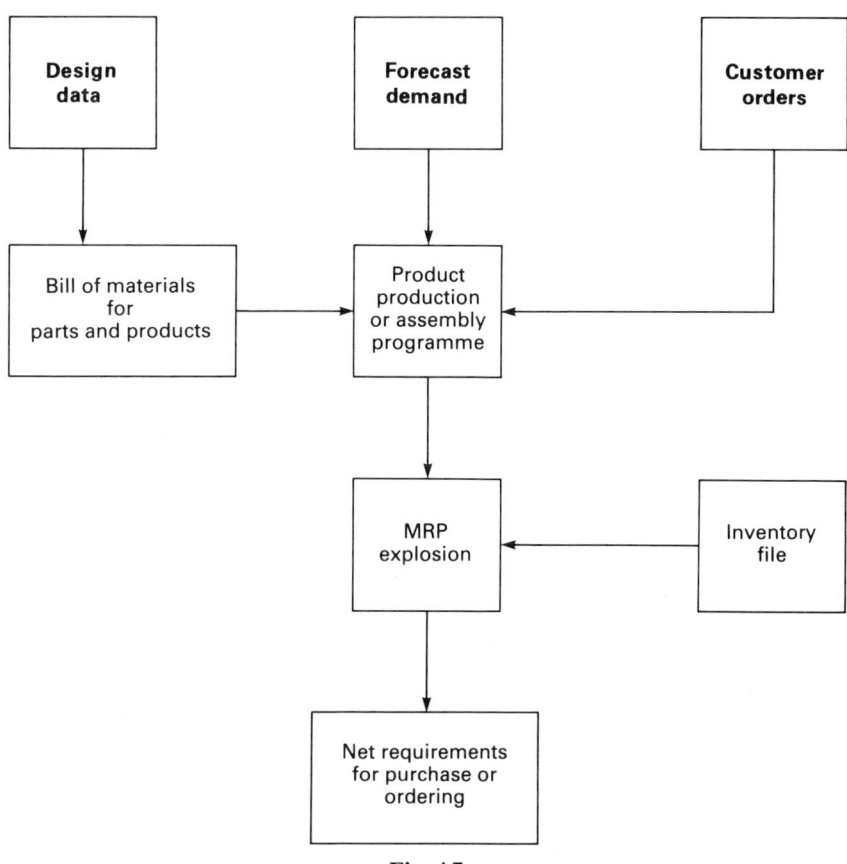

Fig. 4.7

ITEM INFORMATION

The main index here is the part number. Each item contained on the file has a unique number—one and only one for every item. The ideal part number is made up of only numerical data and uses the fewest digits that are practical.

As organizations grow, so too do the number of parts and materials and it is not uncommon to find huge strings of numbers and letters used in a complicated and cumbersome way, often using more than one numbering system at once.

It is better if the part number can be made partly from numbers which have some meaning (classification system) and partly from numbers which are used sequentially—ensuring sufficient digits not to break the code.

Following the part number the item information usually contains a description of the item, the item type code, e.g.:

F.   Finished product
S.   Stock sub-assembly
A.   Sub-assembly
P.   Purchased part
M.   Purchased raw material
C.   Part manufactured internally

The unit of measure is usually held on this file, e.g., each item, metre, kilogram, etc., plus standard cost data, lead time, stores location, and so on.

BOM STRUCTURES

The second aspect of a BOM is the product structure information. This defines the relationship between the present items and their components. It starts with the product and defines the sub-assemblies, parts or components and materials that make up the product at the first level down. One product structure record is needed for each relationship. The structure then comes down to the other level down—second, third, and so on.

Low level coding

Within the BOM, once the parts information and the structure relationships are added, the computer will calculate the 'low level coding'. This is defined as the lowest level at which the item appears in the BOM. If a part appears at the first level below the product assembly, the low level code is level 1 (the assembly is designated level 0). If the same parts occur again at the third level down—level 2—then the low level code will be level 2.

The reasons for low level coding are the following:

1. If it is necessary to combine the demand for the same part, the computer needs to know the level at which to summarize the information.

2. Parts at the higher level are usually needed at a later time than at the lower level. So, for instance, if stock were allocated at the higher level demand (needed later) there may be no free stock for the earlier request of a lower level demand.

3. When performing a 'roll-up' of costs, instead of exploding from the top, costing calculations within a BOM start from the low level code for each part, then 'roll-up' from there.

STRUCTURING BILL OF MATERIALS

Careful structuring of a BOM has to be clearly defined within a computer system, as it is at the 'heart' of the latest systems applied to manufacturing. Careful definition is therefore necessary.

Parts listing

A parts list contains all the items that make up an assembly—parts, components or materials. All the parts are listed regardless of the levels at which they occur. A parts list normally includes the part number, description and the quantity required for assembly.

A parts list is not the best structure definition for production control purposes. For instance, in the manufacture of a crane—a large structure with motors, steel sections, gearbox, cable, hooks, driver's cabin, etc.—all the parts and sub-assemblies are not needed at the same time. The structure needs defining according to the needs of planning and control purposes.

Family tree

This is a useful way of describing a structure for each product. It shows all the levels from the final product through the sub-assemblies to parts, components, to the raw materials and includes all purchased and manufactured items. It has uses in defining how to structure a BOM file on the computer and for leading to studies on manufacturing operations, standardization and simplification.

SINGLE LEVEL BOM

This gets its name because it contains only the parent and its immediate components (which could be sub-assemblies, parts or materials) for only one level down.

It may represent not only the final assembly and its immediate components, but also any assembly. This is important because any one of the single level structures may be held on computer file, but used on a variety of products which use common assemblies. In this case, the BOM would only be stored once in the computer file and retrieved when the computer requires the information.

A 'phantom assembly' can also be used in such a structure. For instance in a large assembly the structure may need defining in stages. The parent is the same, but the structure needs defining in separate modules. To accomplish this a 'phantom' parent with a separate part number is generated for each module. This kind of structure could apply in track-based assembly—such as with the manufacture of automobiles, washing machines, trucks, cookers, and so on. These are sometimes called 'generic' BOMs.

MULTI-LEVEL OR INDENTED BOM

This represents the complete structure for a product—such as in the family tree—but is a numerical representation rather than a pictorial one. The quantity for each part at each level in the structure is shown separately. The part number is usually indented, as shown in Table 4.4.

Table 4.4   Indented BOM

Part number	Description	Quantity
1001	Assembly	1
2001	Sub-assembly A	1
3001	Part X	2
3002	Part Y	1
3003	Material Z	0.2 metres
2002	Sub-assembly B	1
3002	Part Y	1
3004	Part W	1
3005	Sub-assembly C	1
4001	Part V	2
4002	Material T	0.1 kg

Table 4.4 shows that part number 3002 occurs on two different assemblies. For the sake of clarity the first digit in the part number shows the level—this would not be the case in practice because a particular part could occur at more than one level in the structure.

SUMMARIZED BOM

This is similar to the multilevel BOM, but summarizes the quantities for each part at the lowest level code in the structure. A particular part will only occur once summarized—the quantity per unit product in the total needed regardless of the stage it is needed.

90

PARTICLE BOMs

It is often necessary to define structures in stages to permit advance release of some details before design work is completed. This is so that initial production can begin. Items other than direct materials or parts can be provided in such a BOM, e.g., solvents in pharmaceutical, food, gas or chemical process operations; or tooling.

ENGINEERING CHANGE CONTROL

Because of the importance of BOMs to the whole of the manufacturing company, a necessary step is to include a special program to handle engineering design changes.

In many of the more modern industries such as in electronics, coping with design changes can be very difficult. Needless to say it needs to be done clearly, promptly and accurately, so that all employees know exactly what they are supposed to do from management, planners, buyers, supervisors to the shop-floor workers.

Engineering changes result from a number of reasons—product improvement, new improved parts being available (such as microelectronic chips replacing individual electronic components), parts design changes caused by more modern methods of manufacture and value analysis, quality improvement, including standardization of materials such as with modified BS specification.

EFFECTIVITY DATES

These are the dates held on the computer file when the design change takes place, which is entered into the product structure file for both the new and the old components. At and after the date in question the computer will modify the plans and records to take into account the engineering change.

In some cases engineering change can be a temporary one in order to overcome some short-term difficulty. It may need to be introduced at once (including the recall of faulty parts already assembled and even sold); alternatively, it could be introduced when the existing supply of parts is used up or at a minimum cost figure (including costs of retooling, obsolescence) or with a block change (altogether for all items that need changing), certain considerations have to apply with engineering change control. For example, if batching rules are used these would have to be placed into the change point; as would lead times for manufacture as bought-in items; and stocks including the zeroing of safety stocks need to be taken into account.

Serial numbering may be needed in the manufacture of consumer products such as washing machines and automobiles:

1. To keep records of what changes have taken place to which products.
2. To identify what spare parts may be needed.

TRACEABILITY

In many companies, especially those who supply Ministry of Defence contracts, traceability is necessary and this can be defined in the BOM (an alternative is to use manual systems or microfilming techniques). Not only have design changes to be recorded but also the batch identification within the processes and the source material batch and supplier have to be identified.

In computer terms, this can be expensive because it involves storing considerable volumes of data on history files. Retrieval of that kind of information may also be more time consuming.

TIME PHASING OF MRP

The requirements calculations from a BOM are usually made in discrete portions of time called 'buckets'. The precision of the MRP will be determined by the time period selected. It is usual to plan in weeks (using week numbers) or in days (called buckets) but rarely in months. In some cases MRP can be calculated without reference to time periods.

MRP SYSTEM PROCEDURE

An explosion from the parent to the components is known as the requirement explosion. If commonality of parts or materials exists for different products, these can be sorted and amalgamated by the computer programs. The quantities required of the parent and the time periods have to be specified for the MRP run. In other more up-to-date systems, this is specified with the master production schedule (MPS).

Data provided in a screen-based display usually indicate the following:

1. *Heading information* This contains a considerable amount of data about the part—part number, description, quantity on hand, unit of measure, ABC classification, made or bought, batching, rule reference, standard lead time, planner code, and usually quite a lot of other data as well.

2. *Time period sequence* Usually a horizontal matrix heading using week numbers and sometimes a past due box, e.g.:

Past Due	Week 47	48	49	50	51	etc.

3. *Requirements* The calculated requirements for each time period.

4. *Stocks in hand* Many MRP programs deduct safety stocks and allocated quantities from current stocks to start the MRP netting. But others do not follow this procedure.

5. *Orders on hand*

6. *Projected available quantities* For each time period.

7. *Planned order due* This shows the *need* to plan orders in the appropriate time box. This is the schedule for the order quantities to be received—made or bought out.

The conventional MRP display would show each item separately, the same information can be printed in detail or in summarized form. The exact designation would have to be discussed and arranged with the computer system specialists.

VARIATIONS ON MRP SYSTEMS

There is a considerable difference between MRP systems—from simple BOM files (containing only the basic information needed and not a wide range of data) to a gross requirement, not referring to stock and orders and without time buckets. Such is the case with a few microcomputer packages at the more elementary level. The more complex are integrated business and MRP II systems, using data base system techniques, allowing for a wide variety of usage and reports—many of these can be generated by using data base, data retrieval programs with simplified command languages.

Regeneration A term used when updating. MRP is performed by discarding all existing requests and calculating a completely new one. Because MRP run-time on the computer is usually lengthy, it is usually performed weekly.

Net change When more planning flexibility is needed, any alterations to the MPS only are processed and the MRP processed from the existing requirements plan. When MPS changes are frequent, daily net change runs are made.

Pegging This is the technique of identifying all the parent items that are generating a requirement at a lower level. It can be applied level by level or by tracing the top parent from a lower level—the demand for which products generated the parts requirement? Or, alternatively, which order generated the requirement?

Closed loop MRP The feature of closed loop MRP is that the master production schedule (MPS) must be a feasible plan throughout the system.

Capacity data must be fed back to the MPS as must details of how well the plan is carried out. The MRP system must feed back any orders that cannot be completed on the time schedule. The MPS then has to be modified in accordance with what is realistic and practical.

Materials requirements planning can be applied to make to order (batch or single) and make to stock (batch) situations, to repetitive manufacture (when cumulative figures are usually included) and to process industries (when the process is the controlling feature). Because of the wide variety of uses for MRP there is no one best system. The logic is universally applicable and the MRP features needed for one company may not be applicable to another. The feasibility study has to be conducted on the 'most suitable for a specific situation' basis.

4.4   Aggregate inventory management

According to conventional accounting practices, inventory is listed on the company balance sheet as an *asset*. To be more precise, it is a *current asset* and normally comprises the following:

1. *Finished stocks*   There are normally finished products carried in the finished stock warehouse and/or distribution centres. These are replenished on a make to stock or purchase for sales basis. Within this category any retail stocks would also be included. Alternatively, this category may include finished goods that are made to order and are ready for distribution to the customer.

    Finished goods are normally classed as taken out of stock when they are invoiced to the customer. They should, of course, be physically taken out of stock at the same time. Invoicing normally follows shipment in practice.

2. *Work in progress (WIP)*   These are the materials, components and assemblies that are in process through manufacture, or are waiting between operations in the factory. Strict definitions have to apply as to what comprises work in progress.

    Finished goods in the factory awaiting shipment to the warehouse may be a case in point. The total quality of this form of stock should be strictly controlled and swiftly moved. The usual definition of what constitutes finished stock is that received into the warehouse.

    Intermediate stocks of materials or parts, part processes by the factory and awaiting re-issue to another department, would normally be classified under materials stocks.

Another form of work in progress would be items sent out from the stores for outside processing or sub-contract work. Outside work that has not been invoiced cannot be classified as stock, but if materials have been sent out free issue, they would constitute work in progress.

3. *Materials Stock* This includes bought-out components and raw materials, plus intermediate parts and assemblies held in stock. It would also include maintenance stock and stationery stocks.

Materials stock is normally classified as stock that has been received, inspected and accepted, and invoiced by the supplier. It normally ceases to be materials stock when issued to work in progress. Ordered or allocated stock that remains unissued is materials stock. Stock that has been received and uninvoiced, or unaccepted by invoice, should not be classed as materials stock. These categories need to be cleared rapidly and sorted out. Items received, accepted but not invoiced should be taken as materials stock, but there should be a reserve within purchase invoices.

Strict definitions of categories of stocks need to be written down within an organization. It is surprising how easily stock is lost in the middle of these categories, even in the best companies.

It is also surprising that although stocks are classified as assets, the company finance department usually wants stocks to be reduced. The reasons for this are:

1. *Inventory* is money tied up and frozen. Inventory released is money liquefied. Therefore:

$$Inventory\ held = non\text{-}availability\ of\ money$$

2. Reduced *inventory*, therefore reduces current assets, therefore reduces capital employed. For the same profits and sales turnover this equals better return on capital employed.

3. *Inventory* turned over once in a year is money used only once to generate a return on sale. If inventory is turned over a number of times the same money can be used over and over again to generate profit on a number of sales.

It would be really good if we as individuals could use our money more than once!

REASONS FOR KEEPING INVENTORY

Although we may be pressured to reduce inventory, and rightly it must be controlled and justified, the reasons and levels normally given by the financial experts can cause more problems than they solve if they are not looked at carefully. The recent propositions of just in time (JIT) production are ideal in some situations. They are not applicable in the following circumstances:

1. When set-up times and costs are high (efforts should be made to improve these factors).

2. Quality is poor or scrap ratios high (improvements needed).

3. The diversity of the product line or complexity of product structure in the BOM is great.

4. There is high fluctuation of sales demand.

5. Worker or plant flexibility is low.

Inventory should be held for the following reasons:

1. To balance demand with output, where demand fluctuates.

2. To balance demand with output, where there is seasonal variation.

3. To provide a known defined level of service to customers through finished stocking.

4. To provide a known defined level of service to other production departments by servicing departments. For example, machine shops and fabrication shops are usually overloaded and do not give a good service to assembly. Intermediate stocks, through planned batches, may be one answer, increasing the capacity of service departments may be another.

5. It may be more economical to make or buy in batches. Not everyone can supply just what we want, exactly when we want it—made in or bought out. Batching is necessary when the rate of production vastly exceeds the rate of demand.

6. To counteract inflation or as bargain offer.

7. *Uncertainties* Trying to 'beat the system' on the commodities market without inside information can lead to problems. Preparing for a cushion with an impending problem supplier can be worthwhile (strikes, currency restrictions, economic problems).

8. *Unreliable suppliers* The quick answer is to change the supplier. A small company having to contract a small proportion of a large monopoly company's production has difficult problems to overcome; as has an overseas subsidiary with long distribution links to a large Western supplier.

A METHOD OF CONTROL

Inventory is nearly always linked to something else. The simplest type of case is in retailing or warehousing when inventories are purchased, stocked and resold. Inventory control can be an independent function balancing the economics of purchase to the goal of providing a good customer service with minimum inventory. The problem is usually one of anticipating demand, knowing the supply and the quality/specification of the goods. Wrong decisions in any of these areas result in slow moving or unwanted stocks. In manufacturing, however, the timing and batch sizes can change due to priority consideration, but inventory is a result of the purchasing and production rates being linked to the demand rates. Overproduction leads to increased finished stocks, underproduction to unsatisfied orders.

Stocks always need looking at in consideration of demand, production and purchasing rates. The four are an interlinking process—it is because of this main reason that the concept of materials management was introduced in many companies.

The steps in control

1. Analyse present situation by classifying stocks and put into categories that can be used for control (ABC analysis).
2. Find out approximate cost of holding stock.
3. Find out appropriate costs of ordering stock.
4. Choose best order quantity/interval.
5. Define service levels and safety stocks.
6. Introduce effective controls.
7. Sell unwanted stocks.

Note Inventories must be controlled in aggregate before they can be controlled in detail. It may also be more useful to control families of items to meet some criteria such as total stockholdings or fewer purchase orders.

ABC ANALYSIS

This classification technique is a most powerful one to use in order to concentrate on the really important issues in a company. In many different situations a small number of items will account for the great bulk of the value. About 20 per cent of the people in a country will have 80 per cent of the wealth. In companies the following can often be seen.

97

1. A few of the customers will give a company the majority of its orders by value.
2. A few stock items will account for most of the stockholding value.
3. A few operations will account for the most scrap.
4. A few suppliers will likely produce the most delays/unreliability in the supply of raw materials.
5. A few orders cause most of the overdue orders for customers.
6. A few items will produce the greatest sales value for the company.

A consequence of all this is that some items need more planning and more attention than others to achieve significant results quickly.

These are divided into Class A, Class B and Class C for control purposes. For example a company has 6500 sales items.

Class A 250 items (4 per cent of the number) provide 75 per cent of the sales.

Class B 1000 items (16 per cent of the number) provide 20 per cent of the sales.

Class C 5250 items (80 per cent of the number) provide 5 per cent of the sales.

STEPS IN CLASSIFYING ABC ITEMS

1. Make up a table with four columns.
2. List part number or product number in the first column.
3. Enter unit price or cost in the second column.
4. Enter annual volume or usage number in the third column.
5. Multiply price by quantity to give annual usage value (AUV), fourth column.
6. Make up another table with four columns.
7. List part number or product number in the first column starting with the number which has the highest AUV, then the second highest, etc., until all the part product numbers have been listed—the last item on the list should have the least AUV.
8. List the AUV (in descending usage value).
9. Calculate the cumulative AUV—the first figure will be the same as the AUV in the second column. The second figure will be the first added to the second; the third figure will be the cumulative AUV added to the second AUV figure. The last figure will be the total of all the AUVs.

10. Calculate the percentages of all the cumulative AUVs. The last figure will be 100 per cent of all the AUVs.

For companies with many parts this would prove to be a most time-consuming manual exercise. Fortunately, there are a large number of computer programs which will calculate this analysis automatically once the basic information has been entered.

A curve can then be drawn from the results of this analysis (Fig. 4.8).

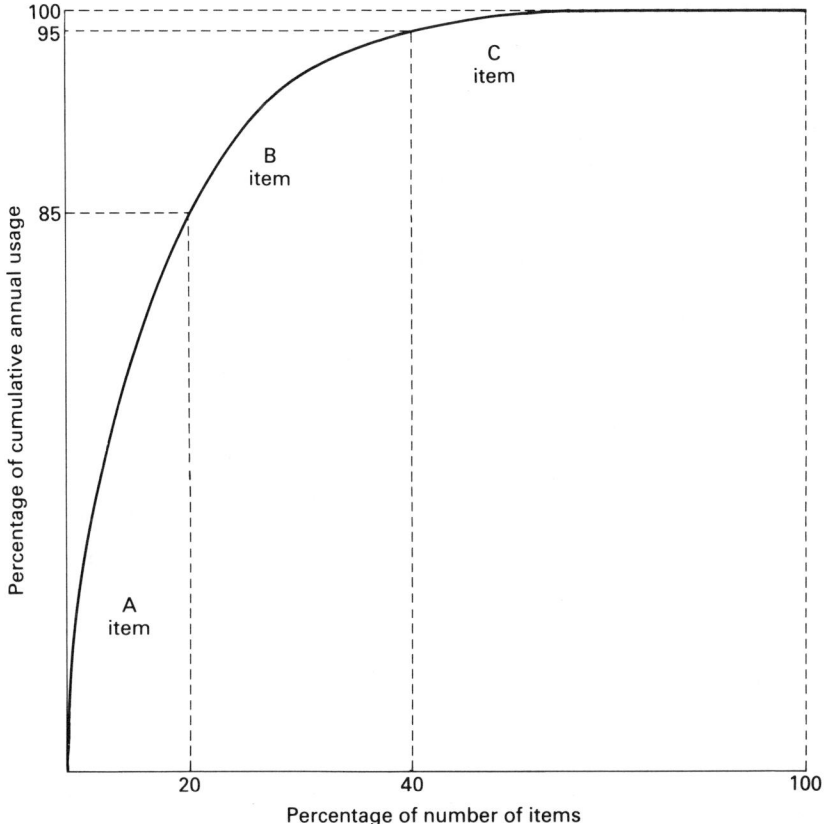

Fig. 4.8

USING THE RESULTS OF ABC ANALYSIS

Table 4.5 shows some of the main ways in which an ABC analysis can be used for managerial control purposes.

Table 4.5 Ways in which ABC analysis can be used for managerial control

	A items	B items	C items
Value	Will comprise the bulk of the annual value	Will comprise about one fifth of the annual value	Will comprise a small percentage of the annual value
Degree of control needed	Detailed scheduling and planning	Some planning and scheduling of items	Small degree of control needed. Controlled by the system rather than by considerable attention
Method of control	MRP and close scheduling or JIT	MRP and overall scheduling or stock control (ROL/ROQ)	Stock control visual review or order one year's supply
Degree of expediting	Great attention to ensure on time deliveries	Reasonable attention to prompt deliveries	With attention to progressing except when large deterioration occurs
Accuracy of records	Very accurate dealing with single items	Accurate dealing with single items	Accuracy needed but usually dealing with bulk quantities
Allocation of personnel	Greater number of people or resources	Small number of people or resources	Very few people or resources compared to A items
Inventory turnover	Quick turnover	Medium turnover	Slow turnover, e.g., an average of 6 months' supply

Note The rules given in this table are typical. Each company needs to decide which rules apply to an ABC analysis for its own situation.

INVENTORY TARGETS AND TURNOVER RATES

In order to manage aggregate inventories, it is necessary to calculate annual stock turnover rates for different classes of inventory—start with finished stock, work in progress, intermediate parts, raw materials; and then later subdivide these into product groups, part or material groups. Annual usage figures can then be used to determine average target stocks for each group.

100

$$\text{Annual usage for each} \times \text{target stock turnover rate for that class of inventory} = \text{target inventory level for that class}$$

Actual figures can then be compared to the target figures each month or quarter and the degree to which these are controlled can be seen.

INVENTORY CONTROL OF INDIVIDUAL ITEMS

Another part of this book is devoted to non-aggregate means of controlling inventory. See Sec. 4.2, page 75.

4.5 Expediting

It is the considered opinion of many fellows of the Institute of Production Control, together with many of our leading industrial organizations, that the expediting function, particularly in manufacturing establishments is, and will be in the foreseeable future, one of the most important facets of management, which will have to be undertaken and controlled by very experienced and trained personnel. So much contribution can be made by successful expediting: (a) to lessening the tension of cash flow by being able to reduce stockholdings without impairing service and efficiency; (b) to ensuring a better utilization of the labour force by having uninterrupted production runs through no lack of materials and making production planning and control something that can be accomplished with confidence material-wise.

Expediting also improves the image of our purchasing function with our suppliers in so far as our suppliers will know that when once they have made a promised delivery date to the buyer, the expediter will make certain, by any means at his command, that that delivery promise is maintained, and that failure to do this on the part of the supplier could result in drastic action being taken to his disadvantage, even in some cases leading to litigation. It also enables purchasing to acquire a far more intimate knowledge of the suppliers by the feedback system of information it will receive from time to time from expediting.

Expediting must never be viewed as a further liability which the company is undertaking, but rather as an investment in which it is going to indulge because the cost of having an expediting section, no matter how small or large, will contribute savings to the company which, when they are all assessed, will be in the ratio of 5 to 1 in favour of the company.

So when we hear the comment 'We can't afford to have an expediting section', such critics should ask themselves 'Can we afford to be without it?'

In these days of fierce competition, with increasing prices of materials and higher overheads, cash—fluid liquidity—is still the very dearest item we have to purchase. All the above comments can be made with absolute assurance providing we take time to select the right kind of personnel to do the job, i.e., people with training and experience in this work. These trained personnel will need to have the right personality to accomplish their tasks efficiently. They will have acquired the skills to negotiate and persuade, and have a determination to achieve their objective and be able to deal with, and remove, any obstacles. They will project the company image with distinction and good manners yet be tenacious in their pursuits. They will most certainly have learned their craft in the art of communication, both oral and written, and be able to make themselves clearly understood leaving no room for misunderstanding.

Finally, they will be efficient at report presentation and be able to highlight the salient points without indulging in excessive verbiage.

Expediting, as opposed to progress chasing or material control, has to have a very different emphasis placed upon it to that which we place on progress chasing, but the point must be made that each of these emphases is vital if production planning and control are going to be able to synchronize at the right time in the production cycle those items which the company manufactures itself and those items which it purchases outside.

This then indicates the difference between expediting and progress chasing. Expediting is that function which deals with all materials and supplies which are purchased outside the company, and underwrites the importance of having trained personnel of the type mentioned above to execute it effectively in line with company policy and demand.

In spite of the many areas of industry in which it has been found that computers can make a contribution, expediting is an area which cannot be economically and practically supported by the computer. We may believe that we can do expediting by computer assistance. We can even devise programs on computers, which to the uninitiated may lull us into thinking that expediting can be done on a computer. But those who really know and understand what expediting is all about, who appreciate its responsibilities, and know the size of the contribution it has to make, will agree that computers are just not economical or practical in this area. The part computers can play in expediting is so small that the expense of producing the small amount of information it can be used for is most certainly not a viable proposition.

We find in some places today that purchase orders are programmed into the computer, which is then programmed to print out the order details two weeks (or some other specified period of time) before the order is due for delivery so that it can be expedited. Thus we have expediting on the computer—so we are told. This is impracticable in the real world of expediting because only the expediter with the vast and acquired knowledge of the suppliers is in a position to say when they must start expediting, that is if expediting is going to be *effective*.

Every purchase order raised must be copied and that copy sent out to the expediter on a *daily* basis and the expediter—not the computer—will determine when expediting must start. The copy orders could be part of the order set produced either by the computer or manually. Many times, with an order placed today by the buyer on a 10-week lead time, the expediter with the knowledge and experience gained knows full well that unless expediting starts *immediately*, that delivery will not be made on time.

With every order placed, the expediter has to determine when expediting will start and continue until the order is completed on time. Because of this, the computer cannot assist because it cannot make these decisions.

We must get expediting into its true perspective before we start to staff it and get it under way. In places where expediting is already in operation, then maybe a review of its activities or a reappraisal is desirable. Expediting does not mean the building up of large numbers of personnel to operate it effectively and efficiently.

Recent surveys have shown that of all the purchase orders or contracts which pass through purchasing in a year, 50 per cent of these orders or contracts do not require any expediting at all. This 50 per cent covers items which can be ordered, take their course for delivery and will be received into stores and eventually put into use with nothing to 'spoil' either monetarily or physically as far as the company is concerned. Such orders or contracts can therefore go into the computer and stay there until they are completed.

It must be clearly understood though, that the decision as to which purchase orders or contracts raised by purchasing fall into this 50 per cent approximately category *must* be that of the expediter and no one else. Of the remaining 50 per cent of items purchased annually we shall find on average that 30 per cent are items where either a telephone call or a letter is all that is needed to ensure that deliveries are made to the company on time. Here again the decision as to which these suppliers are and the correct action to be taken with them *must* be that of the expediter and no one else.

This then leaves us with a 20 per cent residue of really difficult items to expedite effectively. To do this will involve visits to suppliers' works, telephone follow-up and other back-up action which the expediter must employ in order to achieve the objective of getting this 20 per cent into the stores *on time*.

103

In most cases it is this 20 per cent which causes all the headaches and also causes disruption in our production planning and control department and along our production lines. This is why we need skilled trained personnel to undertake this task. We might even find ourselves loaning to our suppliers raw materials to get our supplies to stores on time, until such time as our suppliers receive delivery of their raw materials at a later date and replace our stocks from them. We shall know how we can help our suppliers in any way possible, so that they can help us to achieve our objective, this being done by a close relationship being built up between our expediter and the production controller of our suppliers who is able to give *real* information on whether we will receive our supplies on time and whether he requires any assistance from the expediter to achieve this.

If, for any reason, the expediter discovers that the target date for a delivery is *not* going to be met, such cases should be reported to the purchasing manager at the very earliest possible date so as to give him the maximum opportunity to take remedial action.

The expediter's responsibility must only be associated with delivery of materials on time. Any other matters like prices, drawings, etc., which are raised with him during his contacts with suppliers, must be referred to the appropriate head of department concerned for urgent action. The expediter will explain this to the suppliers at the appropriate time.

The very simple manual system that will operate in the expediter's office is to have the following:

One 3-drawer filing cabinet.
One loose-leaf book 10 inches × 8 inches with alphabetical tags on the pages.
Thirty-one loose dividing cards to fit the filing cabinet for dividers. These cards will be numbered clearly in the top right-hand corner 1 to 31.
An appropriate number of plain divider cards for the other two drawers of the filing cabinet.

It can be seen how inexpensive it is to equip this very important section.

A page in the loose-leaf book is edited for every supplier with whom purchasing transacts business. The page is set out to the format shown in Table 4.6.

First thing each morning the expediter will receive on his desk the official copies of *all* orders that were placed by purchasing on the previous day. He will then apply his skill and experience to each order and segregate them into three categories as follows:

1.   Vigorous expediting (approx. 20 per cent).

104

Table 4.6   A supplier's page in the expediter's manual

Supplier: The ABC Co Ltd   *Tel. no.* 073 671 3711

Order no.	Date of order	Expediting dates				Remarks
1234 1264 1341	6/9/83 9/9/83 10/11/83	7/9 NE 20/11				Completed 15/9

2.   Medium pressure expediting (approx. 30 per cent).

3.   No expediting at all needed (approx. 50 per cent).

The orders which fall into these categories will not be the same each day nor will the pattern be the same, but the expediter will be very careful to execute the segregation of these copy orders realizing that at the end of his executions he is the person who has to produce the goods in the stores at the date quoted on the order.

The copy orders which fall into category (1) above are then entered on to the appropriate page in the loose leaf book by the expediter. The date of the order and the date on which expediting will begin are placed against the order as shown in Table 4.6. The order is then filed in drawer 1 of the filing cabinet behind a dividing card where the number of the divider corresponds to the date to start expediting, i.e., anything scheduled to be expedited on the 7th of a month would be filed behind the divider card 7 in the cabinet.

The copy orders which fall into category (2) above will be dealt with in exactly the same way as those in category (1). These orders will not require anything like the amount of expediting to be carried out on them as those in category (1) but they still have to be kept under constant review until such time that the order is completed. Categories (1) and (2) orders will be filed in drawer 1 of the filing cabinet.

The orders which fall into category (3) above will be entered into the loose-leaf book and the orders will have noted against them in the first column of expediting dates the letter NE indicating that the expediter has received a copy of the order but that he has decided that no expediting is required and the order will take its course and be delivered as requested on the order. These orders are then filed in drawers 2 and 3 of the filing cabinet

105

either in alphabetical sequence or purchase order number sequence as the expediter wishes. It is necessary to enter *all* copy orders into the loose-leaf book so that the expediter has a complete record of all orders placed against all suppliers.

Copy orders in categories (1) and (2) will be filed in a cheap manila folder inside which will be placed a plain flysheet on which will be recorded the results of all expediting action taken from the time the order is received by the expediter until the order is completed. One folder should be used for each order.

Copy orders falling in category (3) will be filed without folders in strict numerical purchase order sequence until such time as the order is completed.

Each morning when the expediter arrives he will go to drawer 1 of the filing cabinet and extract all the copy orders behind the card corresponding to that day and that will be his expected workload for that day. If today is the 8th day of the month and he/she has withdrawn all the orders filled behind card 8, it may be found that a few of these orders are scheduled for the 8th of next month or a month after. The expediter will give these few orders a cursory glance and replace them behind card 8 for future expediting. When the expediter has cleared the workload for *each day* (and this *must* be a discipline which is exercised daily), the expediter will place another future date on the order for future expediting based on the action and response he got today. The order will then be re-filed behind the new date (say 16th) and the loose-leaf book will be amended accordingly as shown on page 105. This process continues until the order is completed. When the order is completed a small rubber stamp stamps the word 'completed' against the order in the 'Remarks' column, the order is extracted from the cabinet and filed elsewhere in the office for the appropriate time, in line with company policy. Folders are carefully retrieved for re-use.

Similarly, as orders are completed in drawers 2 and 3, the appropriate copy of the goods received note will be stapled to it, the order extracted and filed elsewhere and the loose-leaf book appropriately endorsed 'completed' as above.

It is imperative that the expediter receives a copy of every goods received note raised in the stores on a strict daily basis so that the orders in expediting can be amended with the information. In most cases this means that expediting can now cease and the cycle has been completed.

This is a simple, inexpensive, but very effective system for controlling expediting. This system leaves nothing to chance or to memory and each item ordered by purchasing is scrupulously reviewed and, in the light of the experience and skill of the expediter, is dealt with appropriately until such time as the order is executed and the goods are safely in the stores ready to be used.

The importance of expediting cannot be stressed too strongly. If placed in experienced and skilful hands to be executed, expediting can bring very many benefits to the company which have important consequences on the success of the operation. Expediting, done well, is *never* a monetary liability, it is a sound investment.

Production management and computers

This final chapter of the book concentrates on the impact of computers on production management. Computers have been in use in industry for several years now, mainly in the design, research and manufacturing functions. The influence of computers has been considerable and dramatic in terms of the improvements in productivity levels and the effectiveness of managerial controls that are now possible. Indeed this so-called 'second industrial revolution', arising from the application of computer technology to the manufacturing function, has already made considerable impact in areas such as computer aided design, computer aided manufacture, robotics and computer integrated manufacturing management systems. In fact it is now creating a whole new set of 'ground rules' associated with manufacturing management decisions in areas such as product design, capacity management and inventory management. With the flexibility now possible with the aid of computer, batch production work, which traditionally is the most complex area to manage, can now be controlled effectively and economically. It is therefore vital that all production managers become familiar with the use of computers and their software so that they can use these powerful tools to their benefit. This chapter therefore deals with five separate topics on computers and production management. The first section 'Which type of computer?', provides an overview to the range of computers available in terms of the hardware and software available. Sections 5.2 and 5.3 look at the impact of this technology and its management. Even though this is a highly specialized field in its own right, these sections provide a basic introduction to the various facets of the subject. The remaining sections discuss the impact computers have had on production planning and materials control activities of a company especially on the information handling and decision-making aspects.

108

5.1 Which type of computer?

WHAT IS A COMPUTER?

Computers have been defined in many different ways and can in fact cover many different types of machine. They can be mechanical, electromagnetic, fluidic or electronic, and can operate in analogue or digital mode.

An analogue machine is one that works in a continuously variable mode; for instance, its signals are line voltages or currents, and calculations are made by reference to continuous variables, such as a slide position in a mechanism, a continuous hand movement on a dial, or electrical currents or voltages.

A digital machine is one that works in 'pulses'. Its signals from, say, a processor to a disk are along cables, but in distinct steps of voltage or current, switching on and off at a known number of pulses, and a variable measure is represented by pulsed steps of a particular pattern.

A computer is often described as a calculating machine, which is controlled by an internally stored 'logic system' called the 'program'.

The equipment that forms the computer—processor, VDUs, disks, printers—is called *hardware*.

The programs, systems manuals and operating instructions are called the *software*.

BRIEF HISTORY OF COMPUTERS

Computers have not suddenly come upon the scene, and a short glimpse at the historical perspective will help to provide a background to this introduction.

The first mechanical calculator was produced by Blaise Pascal in 1642 to add/subtract tax returns. In 1901 a Frenchman named Jacquard invented the punched card system for controlling the threads of his weaving looms. In 1933, Charles Babbage developed his difference engine, which incorporated a mechanical counting wheel store. This was programmed to carry out arithmetical operations by the first programmer—Lady Lovelace.

The American Hollerith machine which used punched cards and an electromechanical calculator was introduced in 1889.

During the 1940s Eckert and Mauchley brought out the ENIAC (electronic numerical integrator and calculator) to work out ballistics tables at Pennsylvania University. J. Von Neumann devised and used mercury acoustic delay lines to store both instructions and data which was sold to the US Census Bureau in 1951. The EDSAC (electronic delay storage automatic calculator) was built by M. V. Wilkes at Cambridge University in 1948.

109

The transistor was invented in 1948 which led to the second generation machine being first delivered in 1959. International Business Machines (IBM) brought out the first stored program computer in 1953, the 701, which in 1955 became the 704 and with ferrite ring magnetic core memory, this was followed by the 1401.

Later, in 1962, T. Watson, Chairman of IBM, invited his top executives to his ski-lodge at Stowe, Vermont, to discuss the new 360 range that was under development, the forerunner of the third generation machine. During the 1970s IBM quickly acquired 70 per cent of the computer market. The 370 series developed from the range, subsequent models have since been introduced.

By 1977 semiconductor or random access memory was made available in minicomputers by Honeywell, Digital Equipment Corporation and Hewlett-Packard.

Following this, LSI chips were developed—large scale integration of many components and circuits on to one 'minute' fabrication of metal oxide on silicon (MOC). LSI was first applied to calculator chips where high volume sales made development and production economic. This gave rise to the development of the microcomputer.

WHO MAKES COMPUTERS?

The largest computer manufacturer in the world is IBM, with an estimated 65 per cent of the world market (1984). The company is divided into a US company and the rest of the world, of which IBM (United Kingdom) Ltd is a part. The UK company is then divided into divisions:

1. *Information Systems Account Marketing (ISAM)* Mainly the large systems used by government departments, local authorities, national industries and larger manufacturers, usually marketing 30XX, 43XX and 8100 processors.

2. *Information Systems Marketing (ISM)* Marketing medium-sized systems—34, 36, 38, series 1 and 5520 processors and related peripherals, including retail and distribution specialist equipment.

3. *Entry Products Division* For those starting on computers for the first time.

4. *Appointed Dealers and Agents* The dealers are usually supplying IBM PCs or typewriters. However, a wide range of equipment is now marketed through agents and other software houses.

IBM is now at the forefront of computerized integrated manufacturing through systems for design and engineering—CADAM, CTIA, CAEDS—through to production control—COPICS and Robotics equipment and software.

International Computers Ltd (ICL), the largest European company, is a result of several mergers, beginning with the amalgamation of Powers Samas and Hollerith to form International Computers and Tabulators (ICT) which then amalgamated with the computer interests of EMI Ferranti, Plessey and English Electric. More recently ICL became part of the Standard Telephone Company (STC).

ICL introduced the 1900 series as a competitor to IBM's 360 series, in the 1970s and now markets large-scale 29XX series and system 39, and in the medium range, system 25, plus a variety of smaller machines including PCs and networked systems.

Other companies making 'mainframe' computers are Honeywell, NCR, Univac, Burroughs. Mainframe computers usually cost upwards of £250 000 including multi-million pound models.

There are more expensive super-computers available for very powerful calculations and processing. The main manufacturer of these is CRAY. The 'mainframe' manufacturers also make 'maxi' business machines, e.g., IBM 34, 36 and 38; these cost between £50 000 and £150 000. Other 'maxi' manufacturers are also Harris, Interdata and Prime.

The next range of computers are the '*minis*' which can range from low cost units of £20 000 up to £280 000 plus. The largest manufacturer of this type of equipment is the Digital Equipment Corporation, a US company making PDP8 and 11, the VAX family machines and DEC 2020. Others in this market are Data General (Nova and CS Series), Hewlett-Packard (HP Series), General Automation, Honeywell (Level 6), IBM (Series 1), Ferranti (F1600, 700 Argus) and GEC (2050, 4000 series).

Microprocessor manufacturers of the basic 'chips' are Intel, Motorola, Nippon, Texas Instruments, Zilog. Each markets a standard range of processing, memory and input-output devices.

These chips are used on printed circuit boards (PCBs) to form microcomputers of which the following are popular—IBM, Apricot, Apple, Comperq. These start at a cost of about £1000 upwards.

One of the problems when dealing with computer people is understanding their 'technical' language. Most equipment has a whole range of numbers, as the examples provided above show, and many aspects of software have initials, e.g., MVS, PICK, IMS, COPICS, which even when working with one single manufacturer's equipment needs some getting used to.

111

In addition to the above, there are many other manufacturers of peripheral equipment, e.g., disks, printers, VDUs, and many companies who sell OEM equipment plus software.

HARDWARE CONFIGURATION

A computer installation is usually made up of two different types of equipment, namely:

1. The processing unit
2. Peripheral units comprising:
   (a) input/output units (VDU, readers, printers, terminals);
   (b) backing store (magnetic disk, magnetic tape);
   (c) console (typewriter or VDU with keyboard).

The processing unit

Comprised of the main memory, arithmetic and control units, input/output channels.

The main memory

Is now usually transistor (TTL, 12L, ECL) or silicon oxide chip (nMOS, pMOS) or gallium-arsenide microcircuit. The computer works at a cycling speed, controlled by an internal clock, which is usually measured in millionths of a second or even smaller durations.

The processing memory

Contains the 'current' program instructions—operating systems, data base systems, and application programs. It also contains data loaded via input, output or processed.

The arithmetic unit

Contains circuitry for performing arithmetic and logical operations.

The control unit

Contains circuitry to monitor and control all the operations of the computer. It acts as the link between the peripheral units and the main memory through input/output channels.

Peripheral units

The peripherals comprise the following main items:

112

Disk storage

Fixed disks
Removable cartridges:

– Single or double pattern
– Multi pattern
Removable diskette:

– Floppy disks
– Micro disks

Terminals

Visual display unit (VDU)
Data entry terminal (DE)
Multi-function work station (MFWS)
Key to diskette
Remote job entry (RJE)
Key to disk system

Printers

Line printers:
– Chain, drum, laser
Character printers:
– dot matrix, daisy wheel, electrostatic, ink jet.

SUMMARY OF BASIC FUNCTIONS OF COMPUTER

To summarize, the basic functions of a computer performed by its various units are:

1. Arithmetic—add, subtract, multiply, divide.

2. Transferring data from input units to main memory.

3. Moving data around in main memory for processing.

4. Writing data out to output devices.

5. Assessing instructions for processing.

6. Transferring instruction into and out of main memory.

7. Carrying out (executing) instructions.

WHAT ARE MAINFRAMES, MINICOMPUTERS AND MICROCOMPUTERS?

The term computer normally refers to a general-purpose, high-speed programmable machine that is designed to handle a wide range of computing problems. This is perhaps a reasonable definition of a mainframe, because it

113

is designed to handle a wide variety of processing applications (commercial, technical or scientific), and a multitude of users.

They are often grouped into the following divisions:

Mainframes
Minicomputers
Business microcomputers
Home microcomputers
Programmable logic controllers
Microprocessing chips

They range in price from £2 for a hard-wired logic component, £5 for an electronic calculator, £20 for a programmable calculator, £50 for a 'personal' microcomputer with keyboard (but no screen), £3000 for a microcomputer with 'floppy' disks and a printer, £30 000 for a mini-computer to £200 000 for a mainframe. The individual prices will, of course, vary according to the different pieces of equipment selected and the speed, power and memory of the main machine.

However, perhaps the best way of differentiating between the different classes of computers is in four areas:

1. The speed of the machine (cycles per second).

2. The size of the memory (usually expressed in bytes).

3. The instructional capabilities (how a program is coded for the computer).

4. The way data is transferred input/output to main memory and the number and type of peripherals which can be supported.

All computers are, however, complete machines in that they all contain:

Power supplies
Controllers
Input/output channels
Arithmetic unit, etc.

The microcomputer usually has one *common* connection system for transferring data, this is called the BUS system.

SOFTWARE

As stated previously the 'software' includes the programs, the system manuals and user instructions.

The 'program' is that part which provides the instructions for the computer to perform its tasks. A program is normally sequential, starting from the first instruction, to the second and so on until it comes to the end instruction. It is possible to 'jump' instructions with 'go to' statements, or by bringing in standard sections of programs, e.g., sub-routines.

Most computers work in 'binary' digits of some form, and therefore certain arrangements or codes mean certain things. The first level of 'programs' are assembly codes, whereby perhaps 200 basic instructions can be combined to produce a program, e.g.:

$$LDA = load A, \quad STA = store A, \quad MVN = move numeric$$

Although assembly codes can be very efficient, they are not the most economical way of programming. It would take much longer to develop an assembly program and the programmer would have to be more skilled and knowledgeable in details of how the computer worked.

Because of this, 'high level languages' were developed *based either on mathematical or logic symbols, or on simplified language.* The 'mathematical' notations are typical of what are called *scientific languages* and the word notations are typical of what are called *commercial languages.*

These high level languages have to be translated from scientific or commercial program language into machine language (binary notation). This is called *compilation* if the whole program is translated as a complete set; or, alternatively, sometimes the language is translating one instruction at a time called *interpretation.*

The set of programs used to undertake these translations are called *compilers* or *interpreters* respectively.

Different computer companies have developed various standard languages to run on their machines, with the appropriate compilers or interpreters. The most popular languages are the following:

1. Commercial languages
   'ANS' COBOL (commercial and business orientated language)
   RPG 11 (Report program generator)
   PL/1 (programming language 1)
   PASCAL (named after pioneer in computing)

2. Scientific languages
   FORTRAN IV (formula translation)
   ALGOL (algorithm-based language)
   BASIC (beginners all-purpose symbolic instruction code)
   APL (a programming language)

Newer languages have been developed for use with artificial intelligence type systems. A *package* is a commercially available system, which comprises programs, manuals, user instructions, support and training modules.

115

These can be bought, hired or rented. The computer has heralded a completely new industry for providing commercially available packages and programs. These are called software houses.

SOFTWARE HOUSES

These are companies of systems and software specialists, with consultants offering a comprehensive service to computer users. It is relatively more important today to have the relevant up-to-date software than it is to have a particular make of machine.

Examples of some of these companies are Cincom, Logica and Hoskyns. Often they are linked with a computer bureau when hardware and software services are 'pay as you use', or equipment and software can be installed into a company—the hardware being composed of different manufacturers' equipment (e.g., PDP processor, CDC disks, Centronic printers) to provide a *turnkey* system.

SPECIALIST SOFTWARE

Generally, the larger the machine, the more that specialist software will be needed in a given installation.

Every computer will need some form of operating system which can comprise some form of basic control over a computer system called an *executive* or *system support program* (SSP). The SSP executes programs, processes, commands data from peripherals and manages the disk or diskette storage system.

It can also:

1. Run more than one job at a time (multi-programming).

2. Save information for later printing (spooling).

3. Allow an operator to enter a job and continue work without waiting for the job to run (input job queue).

4. Restrict the system for use by unauthorized persons (security).

5. Perform some basic functions, such as deleting, sorting or copying a file (system utilities).

6. Prepare basic assembler programs for execution (overlay linkage editor).

COMMUNICATIONS SOFTWARE

This is specialist software for transmitting and controlling information or instructions through telecommunication lines or channels.

116

It can be used for such functions as:

1. Interactive applications processing (real-time–on line computing).

2. Remote batch transfer or summary data.

3. Submission of jobs to a host for processing.

4. Enquiry and update of master files resident at other locations.

DATA BASE MANAGEMENT SOFTWARE (DBMS)

Much has been written about *data bases* and *management information systems* and often the contents of computer disk files will be called data bases; and perhaps most computer reporting and output can be called management information systems (MIS).

However, in the more technical sense, DBMS is a software product which assists in implementation, change and expansion of applications that use and maintain large centralized information files and, increasingly, decentralized, distributed files as well.

It is not entirely confined to large centralized information files, because it should be *modular and evolutionary*—the ability to start from small beginnings and work upwards. There should be *data independence*—application programs not related to records of data, only to data elements (fields).

DBMS systems can be either *hierarchical*—when the data is stored in the form of a structure with different levels and subdivisions and is more appropriate to conventional batch d.p. work—or *relational*—when tables of relationships are used to store data. These types of data bases are more applicable to real-time processing, when data retrieval is important.

Examples of DBMS are:

IBM 'IMS/VS'
CINCOM, 'TOTAL'
PICK (relational data base)

5.2 The impact of high technology

There is no doubt that computers are going to make an ever-increasing impact on commercial and industrial activities in the future. From the one large machine housed in modern, air-conditioned, security-proof rooms, we are now seeing much smaller computers being used for a multitude of different uses:

1. They may be driving robots on an assembly line.

2. They assist machines to operate with computerized numerically controlled (CNC) equipment.

117

3. They are used in communication systems, which network a whole company, or even a country.

4. They assist in office work, such as text processing.

5. They monitor the results of experimentation in a laboratory.

6. They work out the complex materials and parts requirements for manufacturing.

7. They produce a whole host of administrative displays or reports for accounting, commercial and management uses.

8. They aid the engineering design of products or prototypes.

The list could be almost continuous.

We have all read articles and seen programmes on the television about the 'micro-revolution' and its impact on jobs, unemployment and our economic prospects. Perhaps some of this is misdirected, but there are elements of truth in many of the suppositions.

There is no doubt that we are going to use microelectronics to undertake many of the unskilled and semi-skilled tasks now done by human hands; the same technologies are going to be used even more in providing assistance to the more highly skilled jobs of economists, managers and strategists in their analysis, formulative and planning work.

We must have information to manage our tasks better. However, for decision purposes, it is more important to have relevant and timely information about what is happening 'outside' the organization as well as 'inside'. Not all of this information will come from computers—information comes from a multitude of sources—some of that information comes to us as data, and often from computers.

Perhaps one of the biggest trends in most developed countries today has been the mammoth growth of the number of people employed in administrative and office work.

If we look around the United Kingdom, typical of most developed economies, we see some startling trends:

1. The huge increase in urban development of tower-block offices for corporate, regional or area activities.

2. The rapid rise in the number of banks, building societies and insurance offices in our towns.

3. The large increases in administration linked to education, social services and central government.

4. In manufacturing, one often sees fewer people on the shop floor, but more people in the office.

118

Administrative work which now includes all clerical, managerial and other office tasks, comprises about 65 per cent of the total number of jobs in the United Kingdom. The total employed labour force for the country is approximately 25 million.

There has been a continuing trend of more and more administrative jobs since the sixties: whether this will continue in the wake of the present circumstances is by no means certain.

The main trends since the sixties have been the following:

1. Agriculture losing 445 000 people.

2. Manufacture losing 1 213 000 people.

3. Central government gaining 500 000 people (mostly NHS).

4. Local government gaining 1 100 000 people (mostly education).

Perhaps the most important point to make is that the large changes taking place, with approximately 3 million unemployed, are the result of world economic changes, structural changes taking place in our society, and so far *not* as a result of computers and microelectronics. It is significant that administration is increasing—computers don't seem to have made an impact up until now.

In fact no real investment in office work has yet taken place. For instance at one time agriculture was the employer of the largest number of people; but improved technology and mechanization have increased productivity and reduced the proportion of workers employed in that sector. The average investment per farm worker in the United Kingdom is £17 000; for a factory worker in manufacturing it is £12 500; but for an office worker the figure is £1500 (BIC pen, pencil, typewriter, calculator, desk and filing cabinet).

Another important trend is the fact that the typical unskilled office worker costs an annual figure of about £5000 if the overhead costs of employment are included. These costs are rising at approximately 20 per cent per annum. The costs of buying computers have been reducing dramatically during the past five years. The economic advantage of using more computers and employing fewer people will become stronger as time proceeds.

The major increase in employment has been in 'specialist support groups' such as computer services, accountancy, engineering and technical services, legal, marketing, training, management services (work study O&M), customer services, personnel consultants and the like.

These all:

1. Help others do their jobs better (or should).

2. Produce information.

3. Are usually members of a professional institute.

They are labour intensive, but how effectively are these people used? Is their productivity of a high order? Perhaps this is one area where computers could do some real work.

WHERE ARE THEY USED?

The total use of computers spreads to nearly every facet of society today—military security surveillance systems, telecommunications networks, air transport, communication and police control systems, electric power generating control, control of industrial processes, satellite control systems and in social administration, such as banks, insurance, taxation, salary and commercial transactions.

There are now thousands of high street shops selling £1200 micros for small applications, and £120–£500 personal computers. The microchip is used in a wide variety of consumer appliances for controlling their operation—such as TV, video recorder, hi-fi, oven timer, central heating systems, air conditioning, burglar alarms, plus toys and games.

INDUSTRIAL AND COMMERCIAL APPLICATIONS

The main application areas can be summarized into the following groups:

Commercial transactions
Management information
Scientific and technical calculations
Instrumentation and control

Commercial transactions

These were among the first commercial uses of computers, whereby the accounting functions and payrolls were produced on computers with punched card input and by printers which churned out pages and pages of reports and transactions.

Most of these transactions are now performed by entering basic information through a visual display unit (VDU) and by enquiry on master files of up-to-the-minute records of all the transactions that have taken place.

Examples of typical commercial transactions are:

1. *Order entry systems* Receipt of an order, stock enquiry, invoice and delivery note printing for items available.

2. *Accounting systems* Sales ledger entries of invoices and cash receipts, purchase ledger and nominal entries.

120

3. *Payroll systems* Payroll including bonus calculations, PAYE and other deductions, employee tax returns.

Computerized transaction processing has taken over the business administrative jobs normally performed by people, perhaps using some form of office equipment such as a typewriter, accounting machine, kardex records, etc. It was soon learned that one advantage of the computer was that it would analyse the data arising from a commercial transaction at little extra cost—manual analysis of data is very costly and time-consuming.

Management information

The extraction of data from commercial transactions gave management much better information on how the business was progressing:

1. *Order analysis* By product, product group, market, of quantity, value and profitability.
2. *Debtor analysis* By customer of total value outstanding, age analysis, compared to credit limits and previous business column, etc.

As computers were improved so other information systems were developed for stock control, material requirements planning, purchasing, shop floor scheduling and control.

However, management needs information about what may happen in the future—most likely events, particularly when cash and financial control are becoming more and more important. Budgets, goals, forecasts, targets and standards are set for whatever type of event is expected, and actual results compared to such plans. 'Management by exception' reports could then be produced depending on what was important to control.

This was developed into the concept of 'modelling' which is the projection forward of likely events and asking 'What if?' questions, which could be produced back for immediate action. It is possible to show 'financial' and other implications of management decision to simulate what was likely to happen in the real business world; a testing of the possible consequence of a given possible decision.

Scientific and technical calculations

Scientific and engineering calculations have been made on computers for many years. For instance, in the manufacture of large electric motors or generators it is possible to enter a few basic characteristics such as voltage, power required, speed and a few other details, for the computer to produce a basic design of size, shape, number of windings, amount of material required, costs and output characteristics.

121

The computer has always been useful in making mathematical calculations which, in previous decades would not only have been extremely time-consuming, but in many cases almost physically impossible.

Today, computers will produce drawings, maps, specifications, tables of characteristics, graphs, and even show the shape of a design from many varying angles and in differing colours!

Computer aided design is now very much part of any significant design and draughting office.

Instrumentation and control

This is a very wide area of use for computers. Whereas in engineering of a previous decade it was man who read dials, meters, gauges for temperatures, pressures, voltages, and a wide range of physical measurements, and who then made adjustments (often based on intuitive judgements) by pulling levers, turning handles, pressing knobs, etc. Today it is possible for computers to measure the physical characteristics through sensors, to relate this to a known standard or requirement, and then automatically adjust the 'input' to the process to achieve 'control'. At first, the control mechanisms were imperfectly understood and different cycles and resonances could make a control system 'unreliable' or 'unstable'. With greater emphasis on the mechanism of the control process itself, much more 'automatic' control becomes possible.

Today, we see machine tools being controlled in producing very complex shapes, and each job involving different shapes, on the robot lines of BL or Fiat assembly, and welding cars with no human involvement at all. Newer robotic machines, much smaller than the earlier robots, are now performing small assembly operations especially in the field of electronics.

The future possibilities are vast. Much discussion and experimentation are centred around machines that are truly 'intelligent', learning as they meet their environment and making decisions based on what they have discovered, or goal-seeking machines which adapt to conditions but are programmed to meet or achieve a set end.

WORD PROCESSING (WP)

There are very many definitions of word processing depending on what 'word' means. Perhaps a simple but embracing one would be 'the automation of document production'.

Word processing in a broader sense has been in operation throughout history, perhaps we could include the cryptographies of ancient Assyrians and Egyptians; perhaps the 'scribes' of ancient times were specialists at word processing or the monks who produced the beautiful manuscripts of the Middle Ages. However, it was certainly not automated!

Perhaps WP in the modern sense came into being in the late fifties with the Friden 'Flexwriter' equipment, first called automatic typewriters, which used paper tape.

Word processing today is performed by computers especially adapted to office use with their own specialist programs. They can range from stand-alone microcomputers with word processing packages to multi-screen mini-computers with hard disk storage and a wide range of special WP programs.

5.3 Computerized manufacturing systems

The development of modern real-time, integrated data base systems has brought the possibility for managers of manufacturing enterprises to have available up-to-date, relevant information, and through their own terminal the ability to plan and control what is happening in their own companies.

More than ever before, the strength of competition, and the ever-increasing technological changes taking place have presented the modern manager with the need for more comprehensive and better information systems to be available for his needs.

The implementation of computerized production control systems has never been easy because:

1. Most production and materials control systems have to be able to cope with a lot of complex transactions and movements throughout the manufacturing cycle—the larger and more complex the manufacturing process, the more difficult implementation becomes.

2. Many companies have large arrays of products, parts and materials, each related to one another in terms of structural relationships determined by how they are assembled together. This means that not only is there a very great volume of information to be input and processed through the computer—there is also the request for this information to be precise and accurate; otherwise the results from the computer are either meaningless or useless. When constant modifications are made to designs, this control becomes ever more complex.

3. Manufacturing managers have often been unhappy about using computers; knowing of many instances where money has been invested, and then the system has not produced the results expected. This is partly because computers are in a 'black box' category for most people; but also because there are so many systems available today, that no one

123

who has not followed the computerized production control route will have much of a clue as to what to expect and how to use it successfully. Much training, skilled expertise and strong management is needed to ensure success.

Although within modern integrated systems, there is much more opportunity for getting things right, there still needs to be careful planning and thinking about exactly what a computer system should do and how it should do it—and what kind of results should be obtained. But still there needs to be a dedicated and determined thrust by management to get things done.

DEVELOPMENT OF CPC

The main stages in the development of CPC can be described as follows:

1. *Sixties* Batch input, batch processing with printed output.
2. *Seventies* On-line input, batch processing with printed and displayed output.
3. *Eighties* On-line interactive updating of information with display output, some printed output.
4. *Nineties* And the future! Local area networking systems of PC, each section having its own work stations, disks and printers; communicating with each other relevant information.

    Direct links with machines for control and monitoring, all integrated together.

In the present environment, the advantages of 'today's' computer systems over previous types, are the following:

1. More complex and comprehensive software development; better software packages.
2. Menu driven systems, controlled and accessed through menu and passwords for data security.
3. Modular systems, where the options needed for CPC can be selected.
4. Interactive systems, where the files are updated once, immediately the data is entered and the return key pressed.
5. User-friendly systems, which are simple to operate and maintain, with *help* facilities.
6. Integrated systems, where each module automatically updates another.
7. Distribution of functions, where users have their own facilities at different locations, but linked together by communications facilities.

8. Parameter driven; records and descriptions may be altered to suit individual needs.
9. Quicker implementation; each module should be implemented within three months.

With the advent of the newer types of system it is necessary to distinguish between what is called MRP and MRP-II. Material requirements planning (MRP) is usually a module of a CPC system. Manufacturing resource planning (MRPII) is an integrated system of accounting, commercial and manufacturing systems for the total manufacturing company. What does an integrated system provide? And what does 'integrated' mean anyway, and how far has integration taken place? What is usually meant by integrated software is a computer package of interlinked computer programs usually under two main headings:

Business or commercial systems
Manufacturing systems

The business systems will often comprise modules, such as invoicing, sales ledger, cash book, sales analysis, purchase ledger, purchase order and goods inwards, stock control, sales order entry, nominal ledgers going up to profit and loss account, operating statements based on budgets, balance sheet information—often linked also to the asset management modules.

Manufacturing systems are usually comprised of other software, e.g., bill of materials, inventory control, work in progress, requirements planning, capacity planning, routing, on order (production orders), input–output records, cost control (standard costing and/or actual costs recording).

Usually they do not include the more difficult aspects of manufacturing such as shop floor scheduling and control, process planning and setting work standards, but some companies are now taking steps to remedy this.

Many of the integrated systems are genuinely working on-line in a real-time interactive mode—often called user-friendly. When information is input for one module it should be automatically used to update another module, which uses the same information, immediately (not delayed as often happens in part batched mode). Because information is streamed in this way, incorrect entries of either part number, or quantities are spotted, because the information is checked at one stage and then another. The feedback of information can usually improve the system which is operating, often referred to as a 'closed loop' type system.

Another technical name by which this type of system is often referred is MRP-II or manufacturing resource planning. Sometimes this only refers to the manufacturing planning system ignoring control activities, and at other times to the total system which includes the business system as well.

125

Computer integrated manufacture (CIM) is another term which is often used—this, however, is a much wider philosophy than the integration defined previously. For many years computers have been used in engineering applications, firstly in the many complex calculations needed in design work, and also where process control was needed. Computers took over from an operator who watched dials and lights and then operated switches to control a series of processes, such as in the chemical, gas, oil or electricity supply industry.

In recent years computers have been used increasingly in engineering and manufacturing applications. Examples of this are in computer aided design (CAD) and draughting (CADD). In computer aided manufacture (CAM) computers assist or control manufacturing processes—numerical control of machine tools has been in operation for a few years; further development brought computerized numerical control (CNC) and direct numerical control (DNC) to machine tools, while computers are normally used as the control centre for robotics applications. All this engineering development has been completely separate from the business and manufacturing systems outlined above. The concept of CIM is to integrate those engineering, business, commercial and manufacturing systems all together. Some companies are currently experimenting with the integration of some of these areas, but so far very few have made any significant progress.

Perhaps the development of engineering work stations linked to a networking system, rather than to a central mainframe or minicomputer will aid this process; particularly if concepts of office networking systems linked to telecommunications and digital PABX systems bring this about. Much development from even the larger manufacturers such as IBM is still needed, as is the standardization of protocols for communications in networking, for packet switching (such as X25) and for the digitization of the Public Switched Telephone Network (PSTN) as with System X in the UK.

THE MODULES FOR COMPUTERIZED MANUFACTURING

A module here is described as a set of interlinked programs using a common data base, segregated according to the main application areas or stages within a complete manufacturing system. This concept is not a new one within the area of computerized production control and materials management, as even many of the earlier batched mainframe systems have this feature. Because each manufacturing company is so different from another, even within the same industry, companies need to tailor the system they select to the specific needs of each company. This is done by using only those particular modules which will provide better and effective planning and control within manufacturing, and by selecting only features from each module which will prove beneficial.

Companies differ significantly from one another in that some are in process manufacture (as with chemicals or a car assembly plant), some are batch producers (when manufacture of products or parts is in finite lots), while others are jobbing companies (when generally each product or part is in some way different to the previous one—they may be one-off or in smaller batches). Another differentiation is whether a company manufactures to specific customer orders or alternatively to a stock order, so as to replenish a warehouse of finished products designed to provide a rapid and high service level for the customer. Many companies have a policy of just assembling together a lot of parts which are brought out (hence the greater need for materials requirements planning, stock control and purchasing modules), while other companies concentrate on the manufacture of lots of parts through a series of production processes and usually in batches (hence the need for routing, on order control, work in progress and shop floor scheduling modules).

Fundamental decisions about the policy for manufacture, such as outlined above, need to be made *before* any computer is selected and installed. The wrong decision at this higher level can mean that manufacturing control systems are far more complex than is really necessary. The organizational structure of a manufacturing company can also affect the way in which a manufacturing system is installed. Computer systems should not be following through the type of systems which already exist—but should follow a fundamental look at the real commercial and manufacturing needs and policies for any company, then particular modules can be selected.

The examples used to demonstrate the contents of different modules will be drawn from actual examples of systems in use. It in no way reflects that the particular system selected is the best, nor that it is the most comprehensive. One system will be found to benefit a particular company more than another and so the search in a specific case should be planned against precise evaluation of needs and the systems available.

The system selected for this description is the Trifid software system. It is normally used on Microdata Sequotia minicomputers, which typically operate on 30 to 50 terminals. It uses the Pick operating system and a relational data base; but can be also used on the IBM 4300 series of mainframes. It is therefore a medium to large user system. It was initially developed by a software company called SMI, in Chicago where it has many users. It was then adapted for use in the United Kingdom by Plessey, and was selected by the Royal Ordnance p.l.c. for all Royal Ordnance factories in the United Kingdom.

127

There are modules linked to the manufacturing systems which comprise the commercial and financial parts of the system, called business control programs (BCP+)—these comprise nominal ledger, purchase order, purchase ledger, order entry, invoicing, sales ledger, sales analysis, stock control, cash book, capital expenditure application, fixed assets and contract control—these can be linked to a financial modelling facility. These modules can all 'talk' to one another, making information entered into one module immediately available to all other modules in BCP and the manufacturing control systems (MCS).

Manufacturing control systems include the following manufacturing modules:

Bill of materials

This module provides the ability to create, modify and delete parts master data. The type of data used in this module, which is also used by all other modules in the MCS system, is part number, item description, unit of measure, part type (assembly, made in, raw material, purchased part, finished goods or spares), product group code, engineering order number and revision level, commodity code and whether options are needed for alternative parts, routing and traceability. The update can also add lead time, make/buy code, ABC code, materials move code, order policy, planner code, shrink factor, carrying cost rate, drawing number, trace code, location/bin number and a variety of cost data. Within the product structure create option, the issue operation, quantity per assembly, issue department, scrap factor, start date, stop date, and other options are available.

From the data entered, displays or printouts can be obtained for single level or indented explosion, or, where used, lists, specific printouts for manufacturing catalogues, explosions and impact analysis (which enables one to review the impact of a late completion date or part shortage on another inventory item).

Mass component replacement options are also provided, so that alterations all through a file can be carried out.

Inventory control

This module provides interactive, on-line information for controlling inventory. It is linked to the parts master file for key parts information and where the bulk of the inventory data is held, plus other files for storage of inventory activity and history—it is therefore able to provide a transcript of all inventory transactions and an audit trial.

The data from this module provides for issues and receipts, balances in physical stock including planned, unplanned and back orders (an order against stock which cannot be met until replenishment quantity is received), order point, and ABC analysis, reporting and updating of ABC codes. Cycle counting capability is also provided, based on the policy adopted by the company for this, e.g., A items count four times per annum, B items count twice per annum, C items count once per annum, or alternate cycles.

Inventory analysis provides such data as:

1. Inventory classification (type of part or material).
2. Annual usage in value.
3. Balance on hand in value.
4. Turnover ratio $\left(\dfrac{\text{annual usage}}{\text{balance on hand}} \times 100\right)$
5. Active inventory value (balance on hand not exceeding gross usage × unit cost).
6. Per cent active inventory.
7. Excess inventory amount value.
8. Per cent excess inventory amount.
9. Inactive inventory amount value.
10. Per cent inactive inventory amount.

This can be either displayed or printed out. A full inventory display showing a range of information for each inventory item is available, including on order, committed, back issue, allocated, etc.

Inventory details are available in total, by location and/or bin within location if required. Materials analysis for parts and materials is also available showing the gross requirements and costs for each part number or commodity code.

Also within the inventory control module is a production works order (PWO) control section. Here PWO can be selected from an 'on order master file' and then released, allocated, spooled (filed ready for printing), and selected for printing. Throughout the whole system orders are given various status levels according to the stage of processing which has been reached, e.g., selected, allocated, printed, released to the shop floor, parts issued, finished products called into stock, etc.

A large number of screen displays showing various options or positions within the inventory module are available, the above description is only a brief summary of what is available.

This module also holds the order policy categories, e.g., whether 1:1, order point control, MRP generated, fixed re-order quantities, etc.

ON ORDER

This module keeps a record of every production works order throughout the manufacturing operation. If the purchase order is not implemented it can also create, update and report on purchase orders.

It uses conversational on-line programs to guide the user through the creation of the master manufacturing schedule (MMS), often referred to as the master production schedule (MPS). An MPS is a detailed schedule of quantities of products described by bills of materials to be produced in specific time periods. It drives materials requirements planning (MRP) and translates the master manufacturing plan into specific orders for needed components and into capacity needs.

The module can create, modify and report on production work orders, through the MMS if they are the result of either a firm customer order (from order entry module) or loose/firm demand forecasts, or both.

Status levels for production works orders are displayed or printed within this module.

The MMS worksheet shows for each product:

1. General information, unit of measure, level, cost, etc.
2. Quantity on hand, allocated, back issued and available.
3. By date, gross requirements, stock available, open PWOs, net available and new order suggestions.
4. A list of open orders, PWOs.
5. A list of sales orders/forecast demands, quantity, within due date.

ROUTING

This module creates, modifies and presents information about the parts manufacturing process/operation and routing which are fundamental to the control of manufacturing processes.

Within this there are separate sections for work centre update, tooling, standard data/work measurement standards, methods description, machine information and routing (collecting together the separate sections and specifying sequence), including job code categories for linking to cost control and work in progress modules.

WORK IN PROGRESS

This module creates, modifies and displays the work order status throughout the production processes between the time when orders are issued to the shop and when they are received back into stock. The state of an order prior to issue (for allocation, back issue, etc.) is controlled through the on order module, and afterwards, following receipt, the calculation of both standard and actual costs needs to take place. This records the progress of work that is actually on the shop floor. It pinpoints costs associated with variance reporting, and provides a work centre load report.

INPUT–OUTPUT CONTROL

This monitors the work entering and leaving each work centre and provides information for comparing planned and actual performance and daily priority dispatch lists. The output from one work centre is often the input to another, and this is monitored.

COST CONTROL

This provides a logical and comprehensive cost build-up system for each product. It starts from the bottom of a structure with costs for materials and bought-out parts, and works its way to the top level by adding costs of operations, processes and assemblies on the way. It uses the bill of materials and routing files to generate both standard and current costs.

REQUIREMENTS PLANNING (RP)

This module takes information from the master manufacturing schedule, which is held within the on order module, the bill of materials, stock (inventory on site) and orders (both production works orders—planned and purchase orders—from the purchase module) to produce recommended orders.

Material requirements planning, in simple terms, is a priority planning technique which generates material and component demands according to production schedules for parent items taking into account materials/parts available in stock and on released orders.

The modules are segregated into an RP run (the explosion of parts/ materials into gross requirements, netting for stocks and orders), and so generating net requirements. The net requirements are then adjusted by the order policy (1 for 1, ROL/ROQ, batching rules, etc.) and for the lead time of orders. They are separated between requirements for manufacturing and requirements for purchasing.

The display shows the following:

1. Part no., date, requirement quantity, stock available, on order and new order generation for user action. Below on the same screen is a list of the open orders and new orders action list.

2. This is followed by pegging details. This refers to the capability to trace items' gross requirements to their sources, such as immediate parent code, top part code, total lead time, quantity related.

131

Other parts to the module include buying detail display and exception reporting, showing which orders need adjusting because of changed demands—this might recommend cancellation, rescheduling, new order or no requirements.

The Trifid system uses the principle of regeneration for its MRP, which is a method of updating MRP periodically in which all previous planned data is discarded and a completely new plan prepared using the latest information on MPS, BOM, on hand, order balances, safety stocks, allocation and other parameters.

The other method of updating MRP is called net change, which periodically or continually utilizes only changes in requirements, inventory balances, order quantities and BOM in order to calculate the order requirements.

CAPACITY PLANNING

This is often called capacity requirements planning (CRP). It determines the workload by time period in each work centre for labour and machines, over- and under-loaded situations being identified for management action.

It should be noted that there is a difference between scheduling and loading. Loading keeps a tally on the workloads generated by work orders for each work centre within the time period that an MRP has planned for it to occur. It generally takes the overall lead time for a part, divides by the number of operations and loads the time to be taken into a particular time period (bucket). A bucketless system is an MRP program with time periods of one day.

Scheduling on the other hand, determines the orderly rules for starting and finishing dates of the significant operations on a manufacturing order. It takes into account a network of how operations and parts need to come together, the setting time for the batch, the total operation time (quantity × time per piece), after processing time (such as waiting for removal, inspection time, etc.) and transportation time from one operation to the next. Through scheduling it calculates the queuing time of other jobs waiting at the same machine to begin processing. In many investigational surveys of production it has been found that the total throughput time of an order is many times the sum total of all the operation times—generally between 7 and 14 times.

Finite capacity scheduling/loading means either scheduling or loading orders into a work centre recognizing finite limits on the capacity available and rescheduling overloads (e.g., limiting loads to say 36 hours in a 40-hour week).

Infinite capacity scheduling/loading ignores any limits on the capacity of the work centre to handle the work.

Backwards scheduling is computed by working backwards from the due date of an order to determine the start date of operations; during this operation it can also determine float times for the operation, determined by the earliest and latest start dates (ESD and LSD). Forwards scheduling is working forward from the present time and working out the scheduled finish date for the order, working within finite capacity limits, and working out a scheduled start date (SSD) for each operation, determined by priority factors selected for scheduling by the user.

Within a scheduling system there is usually a local report based on SSD, with ESD loads and LSD loads compared against available capacity, together with a 'work to list'—giving a suggested order to perform work for the shop floor. Very few of the integrated manufacturing systems include scheduling—which is generally considered to be the most difficult part of manufacturing systems. Generally assembly flow line production and process flow production do not require scheduling in this way. Some companies have generated special programs to simulate the flows in such systems as these.

OTHER FORMS OF MANUFACTURING SYSTEMS

There are many other ways in which computers are used in manufacturing systems—not including the engineering side of production systems such as CNC, DNC, computer aided engineering (CAE), process controllers, flexible manufacturing systems, etc. The main ones in use will be discussed briefly:

SHOP FLOOR DATA COLLECTION

This involves terminals on the shop floor—using a numerical keyboard and facilities for badge or order identification. This type of transaction is normally identified by the operator (using the badge), the order identity and then the quantity or time booked. The terminals are linked into the computer system for the recording of output, lost time and hours worked.

MACHINE MONITORING

This is when each machine is logged for running and stop time using a sensor. A push-button recording device is used to record the type of lost time, e.g., machine break-down, waiting for work, waiting for materials, etc.; and the whole connected to a computer system which reports on performance and utilization, etc.

133

COMPUTERIZED PLANNING AND ESTIMATING SYSTEMS

These systems contain work standards derived from time study or methods time measurement (MTM) for handling of work and assembly, and process times for a large variety of machining, presswork, fabrication and other operations. They combine operations planning, work measurement, estimating and the production of process planning paperwork, operation job tickets, cost estimates and route cards within the output; they are usually run on a microcomputer.

PLANNING BY MICROCOMPUTER

In many of the larger companies, increasing use is being made of microcomputers within the production planning and control office. Some of these systems have been written specifically by users or computer departments using the BASIC language, but the large majority use the standard packages which are available for these machines. Typical examples are as follows:

1. Spreadsheet systems for capacity planning, master programming and for the financial evaluation of production information.
2. Word processing for parts lists, materials schedules and production system procedure manuals.
3. Data management systems for output recording and comparison of actual results with plans.
4. Graphical packages linked to statistical analysis for trend analysis, forecasting and displaying market shares, histograms and demand plots.

With the more modern systems these types of package are integrated together.

MICROCOMPUTERS FOR THE SMALLER USER

Smaller systems are also available for the smaller manufacturing company using the microcomputer. Examples of these are:

1. Stock control packages.
2. MRP packages.
3. Shop scheduling (simulating Gantt charts).

These are not integrated systems, but stand-alone modules—much simplified compared to the integrated manufacturing systems described above. For systems work on microcomputers, it is better to use Winchester disk files than the floppy disk drives, because of the volume of information that is normally required on PC systems. For instance, a single-sided single density floppy disk will usually hold approximately 500K bytes of storage. If a stock file master contains 500 bytes per item (which is quite a small amount of data), then only 1000 records could be held on each floppy.

Larger microcomputer systems have appeared on the market within the last few years, which are truly integrated packages and very good value for the small to small/medium-sized company. For material control applications MicroSafes is a market leader and for scheduling systems Micross has many applications (even among larger users). Sheffield Micro also has such a system but this is more linked to accounting applications with some elements of PC.

IMPLEMENTING MANUFACTURING SYSTEMS

Many difficulties have occurred in implementation, but this does not mean that manufacturing systems cannot be made successful. The University of Minnesota study in the United States and other studies, such as by the Department of Industry in the United Kingdom, have demonstrated this. There have been many failures however.

The following steps are considered essential:

1. Top management support and backing for the project.
2. Careful management of the implementation by the *user* and not other agencies. While the computer and software supplier, the consultant or internal computer staff may be very helpful, the project and how it operates is not their responsibility. The manufacturing users must take full responsibility or suffer the consequences.
3. The user must make policy decisions about the production systems needed before the computer system is selected.
4. Good training of both users and all levels of company personnel is essential. This needs planning with care and using the best training methods available.
5. Careful search and selection of the computer systems is necessary. Each company is different and may need a different solution to its problems. Selection of the appropriate modules and elements within each module is essential.
6. The allocation of an adequate number of trained staff to implementation is essential. Many companies fail to recognize that delayed applications lead to loss of confidence and morale.

135

7. The systems outside the computer are as important as the computer system itself. For instance, stock recording in theory is very easy—record issues, receipts and calculate the balance. Computer systems can do this very well, but there are thousands of stock control systems which are grossly inaccurate. Good management of stores and stock control procedures are essential. Here training of departmental staff in the procedures necessary is vital.

8. Having a clear responsibility for the updating of bills of materials is also necessary, particularly when there are many design changes taking place and control of effectivity dates is essential—manufacturing engineering should, where possible, manage this or the design department itself.

9. An evaluation of whether the computer equipment itself will cope with the demands of the system. With real-time systems the provision of sufficient storage capacity for data and transaction files is essential. This is normally adequate to begin with, but as more data is loaded and the system becomes operational, companies often have unforeseen additional capital expenditure on extra disk drives and disk packs. Another problem which often occurs is that as more terminals are added the response time (between pressing the 'return' key, having entered data, and the time when information is displayed on the VDU) is increased considerably. This time should normally be up to 2 seconds delay, with 4 seconds as a maximum. I have seen delays of between 1 and 2 minutes on manufacturing systems, showing clearly that the computer cannot cope, and the configuration calculations have not been adequately done.

Manufacturing systems are primarily a line management responsibility; and when developed and implemented properly, they have provided a solid basis for success in company operations.

5.4 Automation

Automation has been defined as the technology concerned with the design and development of processes and systems that minimizes the necessity for human intervention in their operation.

From this definition, it can be seen that there are various levels of automation depending on the cost, complexity and amount of human intervention in the process. In this sense, automation has been with us for a number of years, but it is more recently with the advent of computers and microelectronics that significant developments have taken place.

Since the early 1900s there have been many machines which could have been classified as automatic—whereby the mechanisms function without intervention of a human operator—such as the multi-spindle automatic lathe, automatic shutter control in a camera, automatic feed mechanisms for power-presses.

Automatic processes have moved ahead in many development stages, for instance:

1. The first mechanisms were largely mechanical devices made from the interaction of levers, cams, springs and the like. Many of these were highly elaborate and ingenious.

2. A clearly recognizable stage was when electro-mechanical systems were developed. Electrical sensing mechanisms were merged with the mechanical devices. Here, solenoids and relays based on the principles of electromagnetism were used, together with electrical control gear for the starting, protection and control of electric motors.

3. The advent of microelectronics and computers has developed the automatic process still further. Many of the automatic actions are now program controlled.

Automatic control today can include a large range of options. It is often based on the automatic sensing of process variables such as position, speed, status, temperature, pressure, etc., automatic control actions to be performed—usually by stored program control (SPC) and automatic control outputs to the control devices.

The range of applications can include:

1. Sequence controllers for automatic start up and shut down of plants or processes—as in power stations for electricity generating supply.

2. Controlling the ingredients and mixing operations for batch control in the food industry.

3. Logic controllers for automatic plant as in position control, bottle filling, cap insertion, weight checking.

4. Numerically controlled machines; this usually refers to machine tools for metal removal, forming and shaping.

5. Robots in a production line, such as spot welding of car bodies, paint spraying as part of the whole handling and storing process.

6. Automatic assembly machines—where individual parts are positioned and fastened and the assembly delivered to an output station.

137

7. Flexible manufacturing system. These are systems of machine tools and other work stations integrated with the automatic transfer of components and tooling—all linked to a central computer which controls, monitors and provides information. Its main application is to batch work, where changes in design and specification can be readily accommodated.

The applications listed represent a distinct difference from office automation and business data processing, although there may be links between them.

The skills needed will be very different from the business data processing environment. Automation of manufacturing needs different trained personnel such as technician engineers, instrumentation and control engineers, control programmers and chartered engineers who specialize in machine tool technology, manufacturing engineering, electronic or electrical engineering and would act as project managers for such installations.

LOW COST AUTOMATION (LCA)

Although pioneered a few years ago, as an attempt to get British industry to use many of the more low cost units of automatic control of processes, this is still an area where many productivity gains could be made, and where worthwhile economic advantages are proven.

Such a system usually includes a wide variety of low-cost aids which can be combined for a specific end purpose. Such aids are vibratory bowl feeders, indexing feeders, follow-on tools linked to sensing heads, electronic relays, solenoids, or to hydraulic and pneumatic circuits and control devices.

An integral part of any automation programme must be the design of products for manufacture. This includes, among other considerations, the use of the smallest number of parts possible in an assembly.

There are usually three costs associated with each part:

1. Making or purchasing the part.
2. Controlling, storage and transportation together with unit containers for the part.
3. Assembling the part. If assembly has to take place, it must be done quickly. This can be achieved by the following:
    (a) type of fastener used;
    (b) strict quality specifications and control of tolerances, fits, etc.;

138

(c) Assembly work aids such as specialized electric or pneumatic tools, work holding and stacking devices, component feed and positioning aids, functional work stations, balanced assembly line;

(d) automate sub-assemblies as much as possible. Final assembly should be quick and should not involve rejection of parts or sub-assemblies and rebuild. This should be sorted out before final assembly;

(e) linked with unit mechanical handling and particularly packaging requirements, palletization, track conveyors and transportation.

Value analysis and value engineering are valuable management tools to simplify designs, eliminate unnecessary functions or to increase the number of functions to improve value (for instance, including extras as an integral part of an automobile).

5.5 Robotics

A robot has been defined as a flexible programmable production or manu-facturing tool, largely used in batch production. The name 'robot' was invented by the Czech writer Karel Čapek to describe the mechanical men and women in one of his plays—it comes from the Czech word *robota* meaning 'serf' or 'compulsory labour'.

Today we think of our television pictures of the Fiat or BL car assembly lines and wonder when an electronic–mechanical man is coming along to take over our own jobs!

There are generally considered to be four main levels of robot tech-nology. These are:

1. Manipulators that perform fixed sequences of tasks—these are often called pick and place machines.

2. Playbacks that repeat fixed instructions. Here the mechanical system is manually moved into the different positions required, these are re-corded on to memory tape (position co-ordinates, etc.). The tape program is interchangeable for other movement patterns, and controls the movement of the particular robot to repeat continually the sequence set-up.

3. Numerically controlled robots that carry out tasks through programs written into the memory of the control computer. These are very similar to the CNC program units attached to machine tools. There are many different languages by which the robot is programmed under this category; for example, AUTOPASS or EMILY from IBM, VAL at

139

Unimation, SIGLA at Olivetti are the more specialized, while for geometric modelling APT, PADL 1 and PADL 2 are similar to the NC languages.

4. Intelligent robots that perform through their own sensory capabilities. Examples of this type of environmental sensing device are:

   (a) interaction with weight and workloads;

   (b) detection of stress;

   (c) tactile detection, e.g., touch tape;

   (d) proximity sensing (getting near an object);

   (e) artificial vision and image interpretation.

There are perhaps 100 000 robots used in the world, approximately 50 per cent of these in Japan, 25 per cent in Europe, and 25 per cent in the United States. How many robots in any count will depend on the definition of a robot, and whether it includes all the classes described above. The British Robot Association, for instance, does not include pick and place machines in its classification. In which case there could be about 500 robots in Britain today (1984).

There are perhaps some advantages of using robots in manufacture:

1. They don't stop for tea-breaks and lunch.

2. They don't do a lot of talking.

3. They don't complain.

4. They perform consistently time and time again.

However, there are some disadvantages:

1. They have to be stopped for occasional planned maintenance.

2. If they're doing something wrong, they don't know.

3. They are very expensive—£25 000 each.

4. The first generation is deaf, blind and dumb.

An industrial robot system consists of three main parts:

1. Control equipment.

2. Measuring and servo system.

3. Mechanical system.

The control equipment part consists of a steel cabinet with display lights and a set of program function keys—but inside are microprocessor-based circuit boards interconnected to a 'mother' board. These contain electronic functions such as computer memories, input and output channels for tape-recorder interface and functions for manoeuvring the servo system of the robot. There is an internal air conditioning system because the housing has to withstand outside poor environmental conditions.

The robot itself is equipped with a mechanical system—a system of arm, levers and pivots—which can provide up to 12 degrees of freedom. Each articulation, rotational or translational, is moved by an electric, hydraulic or pneumatic motor. Many robots will have six degrees of freedom defined below:

1. Rotary movement (rotation of trunk).
2. Arm movement, radial.
3. Arm movement, vertical.
4. Rotary wrist movement.
5. Wrist bend.
6. Wrist sweep.

There can be variations in handling capacity depending upon the size of the machine. For instance one manufacturer has two basic models (6 or 60 kg). Up to six robots can be controlled at the same time from a single controller from this particular manufacturer.

TASK PERFORMANCE

The main action which a robot performs can be described as follows:

Movement within a task space

Alternatively called the work area. Work areas are defined by positional co-ordinates and by the shapes or surfaces generated by the movement from the start position to the finish position.

Different robots will have various envelopes such as:

1. Cylindrical co-ordinates.
2. Spherical co-ordinates.
3. Jointed arm co-ordinates.
4. Cartesian co-ordinates.

Orientation of the end effector to perform tasks

These are often divided between two classes:

1. *Grippers* These can be clasping joints, expandable grips for internal diameters, vacuum pads, magnetic lifters or balloon lifters for bottles.

141

2. *Tools* These are the spray guns for paint spray finishing, or the spot welding electrodes. The tool devices are often connected back by tube or leads to paint containers or welding equipment.

The payload

The whole robot system will have been designed to handle maximum payloads at the extremes of the mechanical structures, and to take into account torques developed by the speed of movement linked to the payload and to the mechanical movement. Sometimes payloads are given by contour maps of the task space position.

Positional precision

This is the accuracy with which the robot can consistently repeat at the position of the end effector. Normally provided as a linear measure of accuracy ($\pm$ mm) or of angular precision ($\pm$ radians).

Speed

The most important consideration to the user is the task execution time, which is made up of element descriptions of movement with its component of time. Special systems of work measurement have been established for calculating task execution time on robots.

Most equipment manufacturers will specify movement in terms of linear (m/s) or angular (rad/s).

Synchronization

It is important that when robots have to perform in sequence with other robots or with different machines or handling devices, they can accommodate this facility. The number of input and output channels and the design characteristics of the control computer are important here.

Perhaps the real breakthrough with industrial robots came with the design of the servo mechanism for drive and positional control of the mechanical system. These normally comprise a stepping motor, the servo system, transmission units (arms, levers) and counter balances.

Each 'degree of freedom' movement on the machine has to be controlled for linear co-ordinates, rotational arc and speed/acceleration of movement.

Each motor unit on the robot includes a complete servo system with direct current motor (these are better for control than the three phase alternating current motor) resolver for position indication and tachometer for controlling the speed.

A servo system is one in which a detection device measures the difference between an input signal and any error in output detected, the magnitude of the difference will change the input to the system and so monitor and continually control a mechanism at its required characteristics.

Many mathematical–electronic skills are required in the design of a servo system; if it is made too sensitive some 'instability' can result; or, alternatively, it can be too clumsy for any real control. Different features have to be measured and detected for an optimum solution. For instance:

Force due to acceleration + *force* due to friction
+ *force* due to motor = command output force

This involves the use of integrating electronic circuits for solving mathematical differential equations.

Industrial robots of various designs and capabilities are available from an international list of suppliers. The skills needed by industry today are not so much the design skills, but the knowledge and experience of the following:

1. Selecting the methods where robots provide an economic service in manufacturing.
2. Selection of the type of equipment to be used.
3. Installation and integration with other processes.
4. Planning and programming the robot to perform the task.
5. Planning and organizing the operation of the equipment including maintenance schedules, etc.

This may involve the redesign of some of the products being manufactured so that 'automation' can be made more tidy and clean.

A robot system may not necessarily be exactly as described above, although these are the ones most used in industry at the present time. Other systems include:

1. Pneumatic equipment using air-valves to control movement and suckers or grippers for work handling.
2. Vision control systems are being tested for robots and are in use in Japan.
3. Combining the use of robots with machining centres and automotive handling where a whole series of operations complete the manufacture of a component. These are known as flexible manufacturing systems (FMS) and are controlled by a central control computer.

At present robots undertake three main types of tasks:

1. Assembly (of a more basic nature).

143

2. Loading and unloading of machines.

3. Holding work tools to perform operations.

Typical applications include:

1. Electrical arc and resistance welding.

2. Diecasting machine unloading.

3. Plastic moulding machine unloading.

4. Press and machine loading.

5. Fettling, deburring and polishing.

6. Spot welding of automobiles.

7. Palletizing and material transfer.

8. Assembly of electronic components on to PCBs.

Many of the robots being introduced today are those which have been designed for specialist applications, rather than being general-purpose machines with specialist adaptations. The former are usually marketed by companies already in the welding or paint spraying market, or those who specialize in moulding machine offloading. Very large robots are in use for loading and unloading of furnaces, where heavy loads combined with relatively high temperatures, are present.

Most of the robot manufacturers will offer a range of general-purpose machines, but some have specialized in a few application areas. Some of these are now very small machines and are often used as laboratory devices in the teaching of robotics.

Occasionally, these are linked to the general-purpose microcomputers such as Apple or Commodore. The computer languages for these will generally be very different from the larger industrial machines.

Considerable research and investment is now being undertaken in many countries. In Britain, university departments of production engineering, electronics or computing technology are undertaking research and development studies for a number of projects. There is a Robot Advisory Service for Industry at Production Engineering Research Association (PERA) in Melton Mowbray, and specialist manufacturers are also developing new and more highly sophisticated versions for sale.

5.6   Microprocessors in industry

A microprocessor has been defined as an 'integrated circuit' (IC) or chip (a set of ICs), that can be programmed with stored instructions to perform a wide variety of functions.

Microprocessors are used in a wide variety of ways, usually either as component parts of products, or as component parts of microcomputer systems which control processes or machines that are used for business systems.

Typical examples of the first are the microprocessors which control the workings of digital watches, calculators, TV controllers, washing machine controllers or the ignition systems in some cars. There are even chips which synthesize 'voice' and produce sound waveforms similar to human speech, such as in the BL 'Metro' car.

Microcomputer systems comprise those which are used in business and home microcomputers, such as the Apple and the Sinclair Spectrum, or the computerized numerical control (CNC) consuls which control machine tools such as lathes, mills, boring machines, and the like, or those computerized systems which monitor the environmental conditions in a building or are used for starting up and sequencing whole batteries of different machines.

There are now a great number of microprocessor chips available in the market for very many different purposes. There are catalogues available which list about 5000 different types, such as were once available for electronic components such as transistors, capacitors, resistors and other parts.

Some of these chips are the equivalent combination of a few electronic components, or of a large number. These are normally defined by the following abbreviations:

SSI Small-scale integration (which contains up to 20 logic functions on one chip).
MSI Medium-scale integration (which contains up to 100 logic functions or less than 1000 memory bits on one chip).
LSI Large-scale integration (up to 5000 logic functions or less than 16 000 memory bits on one chip).
VLSI Very large-scale integration (above the figures shown for LSI).

Depending on the volumes required by companies which make up the end products, and upon whether the microprocessors have to perform a few simple operations or a number of complex routines, so there will be different types of chip needed. The cost of these will vary very significantly too. For instance, one can often find digital watches selling at about £2.50 retail price—the cost of the chip contained in these watches must therefore be a small fraction of that selling price; a few pence for each chip. For highly specialized but small-volume chips, the price may run into a few hundred pounds.

145

The design principles used in electronics today are very different from a decade ago. Previously, electronic circuit design consisted of calculating the electrical sizes for a vast array of electronic components arranged to perform different tasks like amplification, modulation, cut-off filtering, and so on. Often one could modify the characteristics of a circuit by changing a single part so that the whole system was performing correctly. Today if one is using microelectronics, one needs to know the general electronic circuit theory; but it is much more a question of selecting the appropriate types of specialist chips which provide whole electronic 'sub-systems' (amplification, etc.) and building these on the printed circuit boards (PCB).

These microprocessors can be grouped under four main headings:

Wired logic devices

This is where the 'control' function required from the circuitry is 'hardwired' and not programmed into the device. The circuits are built up from printed circuit boards (PCBs) using standard off-the-shelf components. Small- or medium-scale integrated circuit chips are normally incorporated on to the PCB.

These are simple and cheap to implement and to install, although they are inflexible. It is not possible to modify or redesign without laying out new PCB boards with additional components.

These can be used for controlling the sequencing of a machine, but are now often replaced by single chip control.

Single chip microprocessors

These are LSI chips which are either of the following:

1. High-volume specialist chips, such as are used for calculators and digital watches.

2. Standard chips off the shelf but which are programmed for a variety of end uses. Typical of these could be the domestic appliance controllers.

A large number of ready-made microprocessor chips are now on the market, each performing different functions. These are then connected up on PCBs for the control purpose intended.

The application areas for these are in cash registers, petrol pumps, printer terminals, taxi meters, engine diagnostic testers.

Semi-custom chips

Often called uncommitted logic arrays (ULAs) which are an attempt to combine the different functions (which need selection for each separate application) on one chip.

146

This is a prefabricated chip containing an array of components which are complete in themselves but are not yet linked together.

Computer aided design functions are necessary to modify the chip for the application required and link the needed arrays together.

Microcomputer-based systems

These are the program-controlled chips or arrays of chips for which the function or control application can be modified.

Microprocessors are parts which are combined together to design the microcomputer.

Microprocessors are usually made out of extremely thin slices of pure silicon crystal, which is impregnated with impurities in a microscopic pattern to form transistors and resistors with electrical paths formed by depositing thin layers of gold or aluminium. Each chip is made up of many layers of silicon and electrical strata, like a multi-layered 'sandwich'.

The images are produced by computer aided design artwork and then reduced in size so that the circuits are etched by photographic means on to the surface of the silicon, such that a 4 inch diameter slice can contain 2000 complete microcircuits. Special processes follow and the minute chips are then cut up from the 4 inch slice and housed on special bodies. These are usually supplied in the form of 40 or 80 pin packages 2 inches long by 0.6 inches wide.

The function of a processor is to fetch (read a copy of) a program instruction held in the computer memory (RAM) and execute it (perform the operations specified in its coded value).

Execution of an instruction usually involves movement of data values between the microprocessor and another device.

Processors are usually classified by the number of bits (binary digits) in the data value that can be transferred between the processor and the attached memory device in a single operation.

The most widely used microprocessors are either 8-bit devices (e.g., Intel 8085A, Zilog Z80A, Motorola 6800) or 16-bit devices (e.g., Intel 8086, Zilog Z8000, Motorola MC68000) and now 32-bit (Intel 80186, 80286).

Each circuit path connecting the microprocessor to the other devices is referred to as the 'processor bus', which has three parts or groups:

Address bus
Data bus
Control bus

The address bus is used to specify a binary number to identify the memory storage unit or peripheral controller device with which a data transfer

147

operation is to take place; 8-bit processors use a 16-bit address (8 × 2) value allowing 65 536 (64K) different values to be specified. A much larger range is used by 16-bit processors.

The data bus carries the binary data value between devices in the computer, an 8-bit processor transfers 8-bit data values as a single operation, similarly a 16-bit processor transfers 16-bit values.

The control bus is used to carry a number of control signals to the various devices in the system.

An example of how some of the more modern 16-bit computers use various microprocessors is given in Table 5.1.

Table 5.1   How some 16-bit computers use microprocessors

Chip	Typical business machine	Address bus	Data bus	General use
Intel 8088	IBM PC, Sirius	0.5 × 16 bit	0.5 × 8 bit	Single
Intel 8086	Altos, Rair, Systime S300 and S500	16 bit	16 bit	Multi
Zilog 28000	Olivetti M20	16 bit	16 bit	Single
Motorola MC68000	Fortune, Sage, Corvus/Keen, Apple Lisa	0.5 × 32 bit	0.5 × 16 bit	Multi

The advantages of a 16-bit microcomputer over and above the 8-bit microcomputer are better multi-tasking, higher speed of internal processing and better internal control procedures.

Very little advantage between the two types in terms of operation speed is given by the following:

1. *Keyboard entry*   This will depend on the speed of the operator, and how well the keyboard has been designed, and whether programs require complex keyboard functions.

2. *Disk access*   This will depend primarily on the speed of movement, accessing heads' speed of rotation, and data transfer rate. For systems work on a microcomputer, a 'Winchester' hard disk is much faster than a flexible 'floppy' disk.

3. *Printing speeds*   These will depend on the design of the printer itself, and whether it is connected by parallel or serial interfaces. The parallel interface transfers a given number of data bits as a single operation, while the serial interface transfers bit by bit in step with a standard time sequence.

148

The first microprocessor to appear on the market was the Intel type 4004, in 1971. This was a 4-bit chip. It was followed by the Intel 8008, an 8-bit chip which became an industrial standard being used in a great many applications of microelectronics in industrial control. This is often used in conjunction with other IC devices for industrial control purposes, e.g.:

8080 8-bit 40-pin CPU microprocessor

8212 8-bit parallel input/output interface

8224 clockwork generator

8228⎱
8238⎰ systems controllers

8251 programmable communications interface

8255 programmable peripheral interface

Industrial acceptance of microelectronics was at first slow to take effect. Perhaps there have been several reasons for this: firstly, the invention came at the beginning of a major recession period; secondly, many managers were unaware of what they could do; thirdly, even the technologists were ignorant of the ways in which microprocessors could be integrated into their designs; and lastly, although there were many attempts at publishing high technology through the Department of Industry, there is still a traditional slowness to progress from invention through redesign to specific redevelopment, manufacture and sale.

The eighties have seen the improvement of this situation, with the main semiconductor manufacturers providing applications assistance through systems engineers, and many specialist consultancies being set up to link the various technologies together.

The leisure industry was among the first of the commercial users of microelectronics in video games and toys. But as with most technological breakthroughs it is often aerospace and military applications which provide the real developments for eventual use.

Products which now incorporate microelectronics include the following:

Calculators

Cameras—control of aperture and shutter speed

Cash dispensers—used on vending machines

Communications equipment

Control systems

Computers and related equipment

Domestic appliances—cookers, dishwashers, sewing machines, television remote control

Electronic toys
Hi-fi equipment
Watches—time, date, stopwatch, alarm
Speech synthesis
Vehicle ignition systems
Word processing systems

APPLICATIONS IN INDUSTRY

Programmable work controllers

Automatic control has become an important consideration in most industrial processes, especially where certain repetitive operations are performed. These could be:

Feeding
Discharging
Drilling
Cutting
Packing
Conveyor control

This type of device is concerned with four different functions:

1. *Command output*   Such as operating solenoid valves.
2. *Signals*   These feedback inputs can be fed from any normally open switch contact, e.g., mechanical limit switch, micro-switch or pressure operated switch.
3. *Proceed inputs*   These enable the introduction of a time delay into a required sequential program step.
4. *Time delays*   0 to 0.8 seconds in 0.2 second intervals; 2 to 18 seconds in 2 second intervals

The more simple have perhaps 24 input/output steps and up to 256 for the more sophisticated stand-alone controller.

These can be programmed with perhaps 1000 instruction messages per program, and can be in different program modes, such as:

1. *Flow chart mode*   For sequential logic and commands such as turn on, turn off, repeat, wait for, go to, etc.
2. *Relay logic mode*   Different combinations of inputs can alter the output sequences and timings using Boolean type logic such as store, not store, not and, not or, equals.

150

Inspection devices

There are now microprocessor-based gauging systems which can determine computer information from up to 32 measuring channels. Such a device can be fitted with a printer to provide tables of data on demand or histogram graphs, or for printing statistical data useful in quality assurance. Tolerance limits can be set and the equipment automatically warns of out-of-tolerance conditions.

Computer numerical control (CNC)

Machines are controlled, for instance, for multi-axis contouring, by 'software' control microprocessors. These are normally used to control metal cutting machine tools such as boring, milling, turning or machining centres.

Many of the new machines in this area are lower cost packages that can be fitted to new or existing machine tools, placing particular emphasis on the ease of programming.

Much of NC equipment in the past was very expensive, and required the use of a mainframe computer to perform the necessary mathematical and other functions, and to convert these into machine code. It calculates the distance that the tool moves, sequences, angles and feed rates, and then outputs these in the appropriate codes to punched tape or magnetic tape.

Today CNC machines are capable of being programmed by direct input on the shop floor using a type of conversational language rather than a special computer language with complex codes. Quite often in new machines the control equipment is part of the structure of the machine rather than in an independent cabinet. Other machines will have push-button editing (instantly to change programs if necessary), program storage on cassette and some will include direct measuring.

5.7 Process control

The process control computer is itself quite small compared to business computers. It has typically been a minicomputer, which is a specially designed computer put together in standard electronic modules for each particular application. Even in a large system it usually comprises a 19-inch wide equipment rack, in which are placed printed circuit boards (PCBs) mounted with integrated circuits (ICs) and other components with back edge connectors.

The whole cabinet rarely exceeds 18 inches in height. The minicomputer was designed with the need for rugged equipment which would respond in real time to changing situations.

151

The computer system can be a centralized system with integral input/output, alternatively the I/O units can be installed remotely throughout the plant, or with more recent systems can be micro-based distributed computers linked via highways to a central processor with consuls. Process control computers are used in four main ways:

Data acquisition systems (DAS)

Where process sensors record and send information to the control computer for filing and retrieval.

Supervisory control and data acquisition (SCADA)

Again, process sensors record information, which is recorded by the computer, and information displayed to an operator. All outputs to modify a process are initiated by the operator.

Digitally emulated analogue control (DEAC)

This is the 'typical' direct digital control application where the inputs and outputs to the process are controlled by the computer system. The computer itself has three main features:

PID control loops
Sequences
Timers

In control theory there are three elements of control which need to be simulated by the system; these can be called different names such as regulating control, analogue control, feedback control, process control or industrial control. More technical terms like P, PI or PID are used to denote the control process, referred to as follows:

P — proportioned type control
PI — integral type control
PID — derivative type control

These are the basic tuning constants which need adjustment to maintain the desired stability and characteristics of the system. When designing such a system, flow or control diagrams are drawn using special notations within system flowcharts. Examples of these are SAMA and ISA symbology:

PV = process variable
FIC = flow indicating controller
$\dfrac{d}{df}$ = differentiation symbol

152

Optimizing digital control (ODC)

This class is similar to the above type of direct digital control (DDC), but in addition has an optimizing facility within the computer system. It can be used for optimizing resources for a process, or could be a combination of programs for co-ordinating action in various plant areas, e.g., energy management.

Process control computers are used in many different industries—machine tools, chemical plant, electrical power generation, gas, engineering, foodstuffs manufacture, to name but a few.

These are used in the following ways:

1. Sequencing, timing and logic control, for example, in automatic handling systems where counting, relay closures, master control and switching devices have to be sequenced.

2. Digital controls for machine tools.

3. Direct digital process control—here the computer can evaluate direct measurements or a series of sampled data errors; and employ suitable control algorithms (control rules which are then programmed) to produce the desired characteristics. Many process control systems have relatively long time constants (minutes or hours) so can be shared for multiple control systems.

4. Instrumentation and test equipment.

5. Control of laboratory experiments and data logging.

6. Machine monitoring systems.

7. Factory time and quantity recording systems.

8. Telecommunication systems, such as front-end processing for mainframe business communications systems.

9. Data acquisition systems.

10. Time-sharing systems.

11. Display-plotter systems.

Typical computer hardware for process control is the Digital Electric—PDP/8 12-bit and PDP/11 16-bit microcomputers which use a common data network called 'OMNIBUS'; Kent Process Control—K90S and P4000 systems; Honeywell—TDC 2000 system; IBM system 1; Fischer Controls PROVOX system.

High level programming languages have been developed for real-time systems such as RTL/2 and Coral.

5.8 Computer aided design (CAD)

Computers have been used for many years to assist engineers with their design calculations. However, with more recent development in graphic display screens, graphics plotters and software associated with design or draughting, a whole new concept of computerized design has emerged.

These computers are being used in a variety of ways; for instance:

1. Two-dimensional draughting of engineering drawings, architectural planning and maps.

2. Three-dimensional draughting for visual representation of shapes and contours, either in a wire frame or mesh generation or in solid modelling.

3. Design of printed circuit boards, including the electronic circuitry calculations and the PCB layouts, including masks for electro-etching, nomenclature and hole punching or drilling numerical control tapes.

4. For process plan design—the layout of specialist plant, design of pressure vessels, pipework flow and design specifications.

5. For cartographical drawings, involving land surveys, contour mapping and the projection of perspective views, map labelling and use of standard mapping symbols.

6. Design of structures, whether this is the finite element analysis of car body stresses, airframe stress design work or structural engineering of steel fabrication or standard rolled sections in a roof lattice or building frame.

It is generally reckoned that CAD will be one of the fastest growing aspects of computer use during the next few years. The Government has established special grants for companies that want to use CAD under Department of Industry schemes; and established the Computer Aided Design Centre at Madingly, near Cambridge, to offer specialist software and advice. This has now been taken over by a few computer-based companies in private industry.

It has been estimated that there are at present over 19 000 installations in the UK, including the smaller microcomputer-based systems.

The largest suppliers of CAD systems offer what are called 'turnkey' systems. Generally these operate from a powerful central computer and support a number of separate work stations.

The software for these machines has been developed by specialist companies, to meet specific design or draughting use, and often will link

154

through to computer aided manufacture (CAM) by producing tapes for the numerical control of production machines.

Computers used for CAD work include those of IBM, with its own specialist centre at Warwick, and Prime, Sperry and Digital. ICL has its own version called PERQ. Those who supply turnkey systems, often based on some of the above computers, are Applicon, Autotrol, Computervision, Calcomp, Compeda, Calma, Delta CAE, Ferranti CAM-X, IBM CADAM, Redec-Racal, Hewlett-Packard and Quest to name a few.

Input to CAD systems, using an individual work station, can be varied and a combination of the following:

1. Alpha-numeric keyboard.
2. Function keyboard.
3. Light pen—often used for selection of symbols and for geometric construction.
4. Digitizing cursor or mouse for input of co-ordinates or selection of symbols.
5. Data tables or digitizers—these are rectangular flat surfaces with a grid for selection purposes or geometrics.

Output is normally of three different types: screen based; printer output; and manufacturing control output.

Screen variations

1. Using a direct view storage tube (DVST) with two electron guns, one for emitting and one for flooding or filling in spaces.
2. Refreshing tubes, which maintain the intensity of the display, by redisplaying the image on the screen at a rate of between 10 and 60 frames per second.
3. Raster screen, which is a digital TV, normally a green high contrast screen, which can be used in bright lighting environments such as drawing offices.
4. Graphic display may be using a 265 mm × 205 mm screen, with 1024 × 792 viewable points with following cursor, vector draw lines, erase and area fill modes and with full dotted or dashed line styles. Display is often in colour graphics.

Printer output

This comes in two main styles:

1. *Drum plotter* The plan rotates on the drum unit and a pen plotter supported on a gantry. Both drum and pen holder move.

155

2. *Flat bed plotter*   The plan is held flat with a movable gantry and pen plotter.

Most plotters would have a small battery of pens to accommodate colour printing.

Manufacturing control output

This can comprise direct NC tape preparation, or alternatively digital information presented on floppy disk, cassettes or directly on-line.

As an alternative to in-house computing, many computer bureaux offer a very wide range of programs for engineers and architects. A few of these can be summarized as follows:

Pipe stressing
Structural analysis, beams, plates, bridges, box fabrications, etc.
Finite element analysis with loadings, stress checks, mesh generation, etc.
Reinforced concrete design
Offshore engineering—structures, wave and wind loadings
Water supply
Highway engineering
Heat exchange design
Environmental engineering, energy conservation

TYPES OF CADCAM SYSTEM

This section summarizes the main types of CAD/CAM systems in operation today, often based on the types of computer used.

Based on mainframes

The earlier systems were all mainframe based and were more pertinent to the large engineering drawing offices servicing large-scale industry such as automobiles and aerospace. Computer aided design quickly followed with 3D-modelling (wireframed then solid modelling) and integrated engineering data bases.

Typical of these systems are:

Computervision (CDS 4000 and 5000, CADDS 4x—CBG and IOM).

IBM (CADAM and FAST DRAFT).

Based on minicomputers/superminis

These can be very powerful machines with a variety of intelligent display and a variety of printers and disk systems, or stand-alone machines. They are usually computer aided design, draughting and CAM options including 2D, 2.5D and 3D options.

156

Typical of these systems are:

Applicon (Bravo—DEC VAX), Ferranti (Infographics and CAM-X—DEC), Racal Redac (PC design 600—DEC VAX), Pefac (DOGGS), GE Calma (P 2140—DG Eclipse, 7000—DEC VAX), Intergraph (IEDS8—DEC VAX), Prime (Medusa, ENC, PDGS, Sammie).

Based on microcomputers

These are usually stand-alone systems and are less powerful than those listed above; the variety of options is more specialized.
Typical of these are:

2D Drafting, Norrie Hill (Drafting and T Square), Midlectron (Cadplan), Robocom (Autocad), Mountford and Laxon (MLD).

N. C. Tape Preparation   Micro aided engineering (MACECAM), Pathtrace and Geisco (NC).

Graphics   Research M/CS (GINO), perspective drawings, etc.

Based on networked intelligent work stations

These can be very powerful stand-alone units or multiple work stations, but limited by communication networking systems.
Typical of these are:

Workstation   Apollo (Domain, N 3X0, 440, 660), Racal (CIEE) and Data General (DS500).

CAE Software   Daisy, Mentor, Valid.

5.9   Microcomputers in business

During the past few years microcomputers have been making significant impact in business, and this impact is likely to be much larger in the future.

Not only is it the larger and medium-sized companies that are able to use microcomputers in many different departmental administrative areas; but because of reducing costs both for equipment and for the applications programs (which instruct the machine to perform its calculations of analysis), smaller companies have obtained considerable benefit from microcomputers too.

Developments in the equipment available have changed much, even during the past 12 months—with new models of computer, better quality printers, and different types of disk drives being developed and marketed. At one time the big names in the microcomputer league were Commodore, Apple, and Tandy Corporation and while these names are still in evidence, some of the bigger names in computing have entered the market place: IBM, Olivetti, DEC, HP, etc. Indeed IBM has now obtained the largest market share with its PC. Since the PC entered the field, most other manufacturers have become PC compatible.

In the UK the main competitor of IBM is Apricot, which markets a range of machines; Apple with its Macintosh, III and IIc machines; Olivetti and Comperq.

Different versions of the micro have been developed for business use, such as the portable personal computer, multi-station micros served from one or more processors and centralized 'Winchester' disk drive, to micro terminals, often with their own printer and disk file, but linked by Local Area Network communication lines, so that machines can send messages to or from one another. Once again IBM is setting many of the standards with its AT and XT machines with PCNet and Token ring network system. While for the single user the PC Dos has become the standard operating system used by most of these types of machines, it looks as though UNIX will be the new standard for the more versatile Lan systems.

Although there have been rapid developments in the equipment, this would not be of much use without the software programs used to make the computer perform to the necessary instructions. Sets of programs have been developed for many different business uses—these are saved on to floppy disks (or other disk media) and packaged into a sleeve in a plastic folder containing a manual for operating the programs. These are called 'packages'.

Packages are now available for a wide range of different applications. Those used for different types of tasks are:

1. *Accounting packages* Comprising sales ledger, purchase ledger and nominal ledger.

2. *Sales order entry* For entering and recording customers' orders.

3. *Stock control* For recording receipts and issues of stock, stock balances and stock valuations.

4. *Word processing* For 'typing' all kinds of work, and then being able to amend, modify or subtract as needed, and file or print the needed transcript.

5. *Financial modelling* A way of compiling budgets and plans for the business, and being able to calculate very rapidly the effects of any changes to those budgets or plans. This is set out on what is called an electronic 'spreadsheet'.

158

6. *Invoicing* Using the computer to record the customer's name and address by entering one number, and then by entering product codes and quantities for the computer to type out the description, calculate the value of each item of the invoice total with any discounts or special terms which may be needed, including the calculation of VAT.

There are many other 'task' type packages, but those listed are the main ones used in business.

Packages developed for specific types of commerce include those for hotels, solicitors, garages, surveyors and property agents, dentists and doctors, insurance agencies, and many more.

The smaller 'home' or personalized computers, are not so readily adaptable or intended for business use, but many people have used these types of machine for more limited areas of application—including some of those areas listed above. The best known names of microcomputers in this category include the BBC computer, Commodore 64 and Sinclair Spectrum. The Sinclair XL is a step up from the home computer market and offers some facilities available with the business machine for below £400—but not including the printer, while Amstrad PCW offers a complete word processing machine including printer for £399 + VAT.

A large number of businesses are now successfully using microcomputers for a variety of administrative tasks. They can be operated by user personnel who have not had professional data processing training—quite often all that is required is a little assistance from an experienced user, close following of the instructions in the package manual, plus a little hard work and application from the person concerned. The more complex packages may need a short two- or three-day course to assist in understanding the main facilities of a package and these are being provided by many training agencies and localized user training centres, which assist in getting started, and to select the better option available. Users get a much easier introduction through such centres of training.

The cost of employing people has increased dramatically during the past decade, such that it is very costly to develop individual systems 'in house' for each application. This has resulted in a big increase in the need for well-designed packages.

The benefits of using packages are many:

1. The cost to each user is a small fraction of the cost of a special 'one-off' program.
2. The software has been used by other people and thoroughly tested and debugged.
3. The packages are available for prompt inspection.

4. You can see it in operation before it is bought.

5. It is usually well documented: professional writers are used to ensure a high level of clarity with worked examples—these facilitate efficient operation.

There are many similar business needs, but not all needs are exactly alike. The main criterion is to be specific about what needs to be computerized and then select very carefully the software options which are the most appropriate. There is never a 100 per cent match. If 90 per cent of the needs can be met at good value for money, then the option should be selected.

THE MAIN APPLICATIONS

Financial modelling

The most popular packages are the financial modelling systems. They are also called 'spreadsheet' techniques of representing data. The system is based on a matrix (array off columns and lines) of boxes, which are then filled with either descriptive information like title, calendar dates, budgets, item descriptions, or alternatively with data—this can be quantities or values. However, the data can be calculated so that a cost is multiplied by a quantity to provide total costs. Specific boxes can then be added together, or subtracted, to produce profit and loss figures.

In fact a detailed budget for total company operations can be 'modelled'—this would show income less direct costs for each product or product group, detailed expense allocations, to the eventual profit and loss figure. These can be extended to cash flow forecasts. Alternatively, a detailed departmental budget can be produced within the overall budget.

One of the great advantages of this approach is that changes to the budget can be accommodated very easily. 'What if' questions can be asked, such as if we had a 2.5 per cent increase in the cost of materials, what would be the effect on profits, or what additional revenue is needed to offset such a cost.

Those who have undertaken budgets manually will already know the usefulness of changing one figure without having to go through the whole exercise of calculating balancing rows and column totals again.

The 'spreadsheet' systems are also being used to simulate the prime relationship between sales demand, production capacity and stock in an organization; and other planned activities.

Once the model is complete it can be filed on to the disk system or printed out to provide a permanent copy of the budget. Many packages also provide linkage with other types of software, such as that used for plotting graphs, calculating trends or statistical analysis.

160

Word processing (WP)

The second most popular range of microcomputer packages are those for word processing. The market leader in this range is WordStar which has a wide range of options, such as WordStar 2000 and Executive. Word processing systems vary considerably in their simplicity of use, and the facilities available from within the system. For simple letter writing on an Apple II the 'Applewriter' is an example of an inexpensive system. For more common office uses page formatting, centring of title, change, deletion and insertion, underlining, right-hand justification and offsetting are necessary. Most of the popular WP packages will perform these features adequately.

Many systems offer other advantages, such as Mail-Merge where there is an address file, spelling dictionaries, mathematical and column adding facilities and communicating software.

Data management packages

These are often called 'data base' packages, the term data base having so many different meanings, that it is better to refer to the microcomputer offerings as data management systems. The basic idea is that the users can define their own information needs on disk file, and with it prepare the disk itself to receive the data to be entered. Once the data is entered, and this can be continually updated, as more and more information becomes available, simple user-defined program statements can be used to extract the data in a wide variety of ways, which can be displayed on screen or printed out according to the user's wishes.

An example of this could be for medical records. Each patient has two kinds of information. The first is master data—such as name, address, sex, date of birth and other medical details. The next kind of details comprise the continuously changing information such as surgery visits, or house calls, referrals, etc., linked to the date of the transaction. Provided the descriptions used are carefully chosen, then the computer is able to search records for all patients, for instance, who suffered 'coronary thrombosis' in 1985. If it had been listed as 'heart attack' the computer would not have included the event.

Accounting packages

There are a very large number of accounting packages being sold, mainly to the smaller and medium-sized companies. For systems work such as accounting hard disks such as 'Winchester' disks are nearly always necessary. Some very small companies may be able to use floppy disks for their records—not only are these limited in record size, but they are also much slower in operation compared to hard disks.

161

Accounting packages would normally comprise three main divisions:

Sales ledger
Purchase ledger
Nominal ledger

The better systems would also incorporate a fourth division of *assets records*. For each division, detailed analysis programs are vital, as is the ability to produce a trial balance, and profit and loss accounts linked to budgets to provide operating statements.

Those systems with asset records are able to provide, in addition to the above, the balance sheet, as well as holding individual asset details, costs, date of purchase and depreciation calculations. Some of these incorporate invoicing, stock control and payroll systems as well.

For public accountants, specialized packages have been devised for assisting in the preparation of audited accounts. These are often called 'incomplete record' systems.

SPECIALIZED SYSTEMS

Like the 'incomplete records' systems for public accountants, which are specialist systems, there are very many other specialist systems available. Examples of these are systems for:

Estate agents
Hotel booking and accounting
Insurance brokers
Membership accounting
Solicitors
Travel agents
Garages—booking, invoicing and accounting
Property management

These are typically for the smaller-sized business, although, of course, larger concerns may have departments which would use these specialized user systems to great effect.

INTEGRATED SYSTEMS

The most popular types of packages are now the integrated systems, such as Lotus 123 and Symphony. These include some or more of the single systems already described, e.g., word processing, data management, financial modelling, graphics and display, statistical modules combined and interlinked together so that data can be transferred from one module to another.

162

5.10   Office automation

Office automation is an expression used to describe the merging of computers and communications technology, and the support this can provide to office procedures. The concept differs somewhat from factory automation, where automation is envisaged to be without any, or with little, human intervention. In the office environment, much of the work is centred upon information people need in order to run an organization.

Factory automation has as its goal products, materials and parts. Office automation has at its goal management information.

Before deciding on the boxes (computers) to be used in an organization, the first level is the strategic one—where is the business going? What are its aims and objectives? The second consideration is the tactical one—How are these aims to be met in practice and what information is needed for these particular decisions and courses of action? Then follows the question of what organization is needed, the number of people and level of skills linked to the particular boxes to support their information requirements. This is shown in Fig. 5.1.

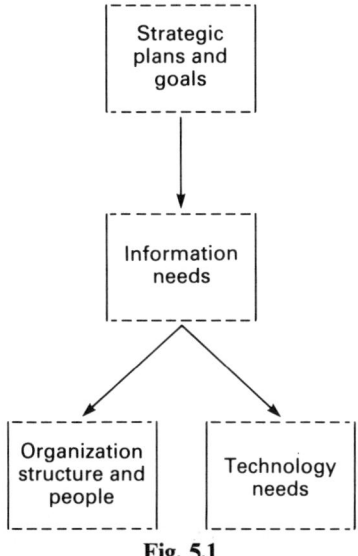

Fig. 5.1

Within any normal office there are certain administrative tasks to be performed. Typical of such tasks are the following:

1.   Image and text creation.
2.   Image and text reproduction.

3. Information storage and retrieval.
4. Voice communication.
5. Inter-office transactions.
6. Intra-office transactions, image and text communication.
7. Analysis of information.
8. Presentation of information to decision makers (planning functions).
9. Presentation of information to government departments.
10. Presentation of action plans to managers (execution functions).

The last three points have been added as the most essential of all the office activities; the remaining points in the list are the usual uses listed as office tasks.

Within the office, mechanization of activities has been gradually replaced by more and more computerization and communication, e.g.:

Filing systems, typewriters, calculators, photocopiers, telephones, telex

↓

Computer systems, microcomputers, word processors, digital PABX, intelligent copiers and facsimile

↓

Automated office system—integration of man–computer environment into networked information and action plan system.

The concepts of office automation are often divided into two main types of telecommunication networks:

1. Those inside the office building called the Local Area Networks (LAN).
2. Those between office buildings, called by a variety of names such as:
   (a) Public Data Network (PDN);
   (b) Wide Area Network (WAN);
   (c) Public Switched Telephone Network (PSTN).

The messages within these networks can use:

1. *Circuit switching* As used in the ordinary telephone system where the switch mechanism connects the transmitter to the receiver.
2. *Packet switching* Where the information is sent in packets of digitized data 'wrapped' within control digits which include the address of the receiver.

3. *Message switching* Where information in a complete back-up store, held as complete messages, is subsequently made available to the desired receivers.

4. *Broadcasting* Messages are sent to many receivers who have to 'tune in' to the transmitting signals.

The rules by which the messages are sent are called *protocols*.

For example, in Public Data Networks, the International Standards Organization has defined the Open System Interconnection (OSI) in seven levels of telecommunication protocol.

Levels 1, 2 and 3 have specified protocols from the International Telegraph and Telephone Consultative Committee (CCITT), known as X25, X75, X3, X28, X29, etc., for internal communications packet switching.

Most computer companies have devised their own protocols, examples are the following:

```
IBM    – Systems Networking Architecture (SNA)
ICL    – Information Processing Architecture (IPA)
XEROX – Ethernet
DEC    – Decnet
```

There are different types of Local Area Networking systems, defined as topology or structure of a network. These are:

1. *Star* A configuration in which each terminal is connected only to a central computer or where various computers act as multiplexes and thence add together another star cluster called a tree structured network.

2. *Ring* A configuration where computers are connected into a continuous loop of cable around the office, derived from Cambridge ring technology (1975).

3. *Bus or linear* Computers are attached to a common linear cable in an office, but which is not joined at its ends. Extensions of linear networks are achieved by having what are called *repeaters* at connection points. The Ethernet is one such system.

Many microcomputers are often linked together in one of these ways; these have their own LAN protocol such as Nestar, Xinet, Xibus, Net/one and many others.

The ICL DRS20 system is typical of such a system, where distributed microcomputers are linked together (in this particular case they can also be linked into a much larger office automation network using the Mitel

165

SX2000 digital PABX and a whole range of mainframe and other computers).

Using a PABX telephone system with digital switching and stored program control (SPC) is typical of the approach to office communication used by the larger manufacturers of computer equipment (IBM, ICL) and communication equipment (Plessey, ITT, Erickson, Mitel), and this is where giant companies are either starting to compete against one another or are forming commercial links together.

A further approach to international or national communications has been started by IBM and others, by sharing a company called Satellite Business Systems. The recent space shuttles have been launching these tele-communication satellites.

Future manufacturing resource planning systems will be made up of Local Area Networks, in which manufacturing automation protocol (MAP) has been developed.

5.11 Fifth generation computers

At the present moment fifth generation computers are only a concept, but one which has made the Western nations take a serious look at the future implications of computers. This is because Japan has already made a start and in 1979 launched a two-year preliminary investigation to look at where it should be looking for the next step forward. In 1980 the Japan Informa-tion Processing Centre (JIPDEC) outlined the general requirement for this system.

In direct response to the Japanese initiative, the UK Government set up the Alvey Committee to report on advanced information technology. The Alvey Report was published in September 1982 and identified four key areas for implementation. These were:

1. *Software engineering* In particular the development of artificial intelli-gence systems (AI), and the use of a specialized language called PROLOG.

2. *Man/machine interface* Perhaps the main emphasis will be on voice synthesis and voice recognition, where we will talk to computers and they will talk back to us.

3. *Intelligent knowledge based systems (IKBS)* Human intelligence relies upon building up a system of knowledge (data, information) and then using reason to analyse, synthesize and find relationships in order to make decisions about actions to take. Human decision making also relies on theologies, philosophies, cultural and ethical value systems,

whole-life experience and expectations, which broaden what even an AI system can do.

However, a class of AI applied to whole collections of information based on the most specialized and expert knowledge available, is then processed by computer to find relationships and scientific principles which are beyond the depth of human penetration to perceive; these are called expert systems.

Human beings are not very good at analysing numerical and factual data, they are good at perceiving conceptual possibilities, where innovation, creativity and motivation are involved. Many would regard emotions as feelings to be disregarded. However, there are rational and irrational emotions which give positive balance to human living and decision making.

4. *Very large-scale integration (VLSI)* This is the further miniaturization of the microchip, and the possible use of other substrates beyond silicon. It could also apply to different approaches to electronics.

The Alvey Committee recommended government funding of research into this whole area; and a small amount has been allocated to specific universities and research organizations, in an attempt to go some way towards the Japanese initiative.

5.12 CPC packages

A brief review of some of the more modern systems of CPC are listed below. They are segregated between:

Larger company systems   – priced upwards of £100 000.
Medium company systems – price range £20 000 to £100 000.
Smaller company systems – price range £10 000 to £20 000.

LARGER COMPANY SYSTEMS (MAINFRAME BASED)

Copics

This is IBM's comprehensive and very large system. It is used with the company's IMS data base and DL/1 accessing language, and has a message system called 'CORMES' to prompt action from users. Mostly run on the IBM 4300 range of computers.

167

MRPS

Designed and marketed as a software product from Cincom Inc., and used in conjunction with its TOTAL data base system. There is a Resource planning system, master production scheduling, purchasing and production control systems. Mostly run on IBM equipment.

OMAC 82

ICL's equivalent to IBM's COPICS; it is on-line and runs off a data base. Runs on the ICL 2900 series.

MIMS

A recent addition to the market, designed and marketed by GIESCO, which is part of the giant General Electric Company of America.

MANMAN

An integrated system of financial management, order entry and manufacturing systems. Designed in the United States and marketed in the United Kingdom by Scicon, one of our leading software houses.

AMAPS

Another recent addition to the UK market, having been launched and run in the United States. Data Pro, the computer publishing house, has rated AMAPS the best mainframe and minibased manufacturing system available in the United States.

MAS

Available from Hoskyns, the computer consultants' software house. This is an integrated data base system designed by Hoskyns, which has many years' experience in the CPC systems.

Other mainframe systems include MAS (Marietta), Inventory Management (MSA), MRP (Software International) and UNIS (Univac).

MEDIUM COMPANY SYSTEMS (SMALLER MAINFRAME AND MINI)

MAAPICS

This is IBM's offering for this market. It is usually run on the IBM System 36 × 38 computers.

SAFES

The ICL system, developed by Safe Computing, has over 100 users.

168

IMCS II and Mission

Two systems developed and offered by NCR for its 9000 and V (virtual) machines.

Manumark

The mark V version of Manumark, unlike the older systems still available, is very comprehensive and integrated. Marketed by ABS Computers for its minicomputer. Earlier versions are available from other suppliers.

MAC–PAC

A series of systems devised by Arthur Andersons, the management consultants. Separate versions are available for IBM S/38, S/36 and the larger IBM machines.

PMS and MMS

The production management system running on the Hewlett-Packard HP3000 has gained popular support in many industries. Designed and marketed by Boeing Computer Services, a US-based software house, with a European base in the United Kingdom.

MANCOS

A series of systems developed by O.D. Management Consultants' main computer systems company. Data General and Texas-based machines.

NIPS

A very comprehensive and well-accepted system for the smaller to medium-sized company. Can be integrated with the commercial and accounting system packages. Designed and marketed by Nixdorf.

PROTOS

A highly sophisticated software system, mainly run off DEC equipment. It was designed by Powell Duffryn Computer Services for engineering companies in the PD group. Highly interactive.

VENTEK

Another highly sophisticated system, developed in the United Kingdom with the aid of Department of Industry software support grants. Ventek is a large US computer corporation.

Trifid

A fully integrated business control system linked to closed loop MRP II. It uses the PICK Relational Data Base Operating System and is mostly installed on microdata computers. An excellent system.

Other suppliers of packages in this area are Sysimp (Systime), PACS (Pactel, part of P.A. Consultants), Concept (Enterprise Systems) and MARC (Deritend Computer Bureau).

SMALLER COMPANY SYSTEMS (MICROCOMPUTER SYSTEMS)

MicroSafes

Designed by Safe Computers for the microcomputer, having gained much experience of PC from its Safes package used on medium-sized ICLs. Mainly sold as a turnkey system by local dealers, it can run on a variety of different microcomputers.

Micross

An excellent system, which was initially designed from the shop floor scheduling viewpoint. There have been over 600 of these systems sold. Available from Kewill Systems Ltd. It has now been linked to a wide variety of software modules, including CAD, CAM and shop floor data collection.

Other packages are available from Sheffield Micro, Premier Computing and Olivetti.

Index

171